My Lisbon

My Lisbon

A Cookbook from Portugal's City of Light

Nuno Mendes

Photography by Andrew Montgomery

TEN SPEED PRESS
California | New York

Lisbon Food Stories

The City of Light

Lisbon. The city of light, where a luminous sun bounces its rays off the glittering River Tejo, dancing off shiny cobblestones, brightly painted tiles, and yellow-walled buildings. This is where I was born, and although I packed my bags and set out to travel the world when I was nineteen years old, Lisbon is still my heart's home.

Lisboa, to use the Portuguese name, is the oldest city in western Europe. From the riverbank the city climbs northward to the ramparts and turrets of Castelo de São Jorge, a Moorish citadel that dates back to the medieval age. From here you can look down upon red pantiled roofs and cupolaed churches, across wide avenues and graceful squares, and out to the Ponte 25 de Abril, a vast metal suspension bridge that sweeps across the Tejo (Tagus in English) and out to the coast.

For many decades, Lisbon was a sleeping beauty, a low-key city that few but travel aficionados could pinpoint on a map. Once architecturally vibrant, many of the buildings fell into crumbling decline and graffiti gangs did their worst. The restaurant scene was good and solid but it had little to offer the discerning food lover.

But boy, how things have changed, at a speed that's truly incredible and, to me, really invigorating. In the last six or seven years, Lisbon has woken from her slumber, shaken herself off, put on her best dress, and become one of the top cities for visitors in Europe. The city is now home to talented young chefs who have embraced their own food culture and opened fabulous little eateries. The traditional places have absorbed some of this youthful energy and upped their game, and companies offer gourmet tours that encompass acorn-fed ham, tasty fried snacks, and locally made wine. Alongside this culinary revival, Lisbon is now a mecca for geeks and techies embracing the digital nomad lifestyle. Artists have come too, attracted by cheap work spaces and, of course, the amazing quality of the light. People are finally noticing what a fantastic place this city is.

These days, Lisbon is both hectic and calm, at once modern and old-fashioned. It is embracing the future with a delicious kind of optimism, while carefully preserving its rich past. Yes, the infestation of tuk-tuks racing around the streets is a pain, the roadworks and renovations seem never-ending, and the influx of visitors is putting a squeeze on housing for locals, but despite all of these hurtling developments Lisbon is, to my eyes, the best long-weekend destination there is—not just on the continent, but probably in the world. There are wonderful galleries and museums, cool bars, amazing restaurants, and chic cafés. The riverfront has been revived, allowing you to take a long stroll along the Tejo with stops here and there for a glass of wine or a *ginjinha* (cherry liqueur) and a *petisco* (snack). Since it's not very far from the sea, Lisbon is blessed with some of the best seafood anywhere in Europe, and offers the lovely possibility of hanging out by the beach even though you're staying in a city. And did I mention the balmy weather? Mild winters and hot summers mean that life in Lisbon can be lived largely outside.

A city of color, Lisbon boasts hundreds of thousands of beautiful *azulejos* (ceramic tiles) adorning the walls. I love to see the city awash with the purple blossoms of the jacaranda trees that line the streets and pepper the parks. My favorite description of the city was penned in 1925 by the Portuguese poet Fernando Pessoa in his guidebook *Lisbon: What the Tourist Should See*: "For the traveller who comes in from the sea, Lisbon, even from afar, rises like a fair vision in a dream, clear-cut against a bright blue sky which the sun gladdens with its gold. And the domes, the monuments, the old castles jut up above the mass of houses, like far-off heralds of this delightful seat, of this blessed region." Some silly modern architecture has got in the way of Pessoa's vision, but much of the glory remains unchanged.

A labyrinth of narrow streets, alleyways, and steep, seemingly never-ending steps and vertiginous inclines make up the center of the city. We call this part of town Old Lisbon, its historic quarter made up of *bairros históricos* (historic neighborhoods) such as Alfama, Chiado, Bairro Alto, Castelo, Mouraria, and the like. Legend has it that Lisbon sits on seven hills (our transit card, the equivalent of New York's MetroCard, is called the 7 Colinas card), but whoever came up with that number clearly couldn't count and left Graça, Lisbon's highest hill, off the traditional list.

Yellow trams, specially built to navigate the tight gauge and twisting corners of Old Lisbon's streets, were introduced here in the nineteenth century. These days you'll be lucky to get a seat on the most famous tram, the number 28, which traverses the city and takes in many of its best sights. If you're a first-time visitor and can squeeze on, it's a good way to get your bearings on your first day. Personally, I like to walk and find a little bakery I didn't know existed, a new café perhaps, or a tiny shop selling freshly made sheep's milk cheese.

I adore my city in the morning, when it takes time to get itself going. I find there's a calming peace in wandering the empty streets after I've had my first coffee of the day. It's then that I notice little details, such as how the black-and-white *calçadas* (cobblestones) are sometimes laid in the form of a ship or (very often) in the pattern of waves, floral designs, or something altogether abstract. The word *lisboeta* (leezh-bo-EH-tuh) literally means a person from Lisbon, but it also sums up the lifestyle, the tradition, and the emotion of belonging. You may have to be born in the city to truly be a *lisboeta*, but anyone can heartily embrace the sensibility.

The rhythm of the day revolves around mealtimes, and the recipes in this book are also divided into chapters that follow the culinary clock. The day begins with a coffee and a *pastel* (pastry) in the morning, followed a little later by some *salgados* (salty fried snacks). Then it's on to *almoço* (lunch), before tucking into a few *petiscos* (small plates) in the late afternoon. *Jantar* (dinner) never really begins until eight o'clock and, because we have a sweet tooth, we like to end that meal with *sobremesas* (desserts). And let's not forget our penchant for greedy late-night *sandes* (sandwiches)—in shellfish restaurants such as Ramiro, we even end the meal with a *prego*, a steak sandwich. The Portuguese love to eat and to share the experience with others; we're happiest sitting round a table and eating with family, friends, or new guests, passing around platters of goodness. If you find yourself invited into a local's home for a meal you should be in for a real treat.

My friend José Avillez has opened six restaurants during the relatively short period of electrifying culinary revolution. His radical approach has helped turn the city into a foodie's delight and it has won him two Michelin stars at the most formal of his places, Belcanto. André Magalhães, another great friend, has created Taberna da Rua das Flores, a tiny little tavern serving some of the most inspired and creative cooking in the city—there's always a line outside the door. Other young guns have followed in the wake of these greats, taking Portuguese dishes to new heights. The tradition of sharing *petiscos* has grown massively; once served only in humble *tascas* (bars), these small plates are now everywhere, with chefs competing to attract diners with the best cod cakes or the most tender *prego*.

Our food, like much else in our city, is influenced by Lisbon's rich history. Being part of a country that was first invaded and then created a vast empire of its own has led to a fruitful cross-pollination of flavors and cooking techniques in the kitchen. Taking its modern name from the original Latin version, Olisipo, Lisbon was first settled by indigenous Iberians. It then came to be occupied by a succession of Carthaginians, Romans, Suebi, Visigoths, and Moors until, after a four-month siege in 1147, the Moors were ousted and the city returned to Christian rule. Another siege, this time in 1384, saw it blockaded by the Castilians. During this time its inhabitants were starving and had nothing to eat but lettuces, which is reflected in the nickname given to *lisboetas* by those from elsewhere in Portugal: *alfacinhas* (lettuce eaters).

However, the single most important period of our history was the Age of Discovery in the fifteenth and sixteenth centuries, when our quest for wealth and spices led us out across the Atlantic Ocean to conquer far-off lands. Sailors and merchants returned with a wealth of new ingredients, such as piri piri chile peppers, cinnamon, black pepper, cloves, tomatoes, and much more, which would change our cooking forever. I believe that the energy of Portuguese cooking today comes from this adventurous past.

This remarkable period of exploration and trade resulted in Lisbon becoming an opulent city, the wealthiest in Europe—but sadly, it did not last. Not so very long ago, Portugal was Western Europe's poorest country. The event that pitched the city from rich to poor was a catastrophic earthquake that struck Lisbon on All Saints' Day in 1755, while much of the population

were kneeling in prayer at church. As if nature had not wreaked enough damage, the earthquake also produced a tsunami wave that came up the Tejo. The fire that followed lasted five or six days: buildings were reduced to rubble, more than four-fifths of houses were destroyed, and every major church in the city collapsed. Even now there is no accurate number for the death toll, but the best estimate is around 12,000 people—a tenth of the population at that time.

This disaster will forever remain in the national psyche but, like a phoenix, the city picked itself up from the ashes and was slowly rebuilt. Those beautiful yellow-faced buildings around Terreiro do Paço, the noble palace square by the River Tejo, are a legacy of the earthquake; so too is the Baixa Pombalina, the grid of streets that graduates down toward it, with avenues lined with arches and arcades, balconies and balustrades. Altogether, it is rather grand.

Another dark feature of our past was the dictatorship established by António de Oliveira Salazar, which crushed Portugal for more than four decades. Known as the Estado Novo, or New State, this "Second Republic" was in power from 1934 until it was finally kicked out during the Carnation Revolution in 1974, when *lisboetas* took to the streets after a military coup and stuffed carnations into the muzzles of guns and rifles, and flowers into the pockets of soldiers.

During the dictatorship, the bohemian side of Lisbon had been buried, and people were encouraged to stay at home rather than socialize outside. The song "Uma Casa Portuguesa," performed by one of our most famous fado singers, Amália Rodrigues, was an attempt to exalt poverty and home life during the regime. "If someone humbly knocks at the door, we invite them to sit at the table with us," she sang. "The joy of poverty is this great richness of being generous and feeling happy." Although I love the way this song embodies the generosity of the Portuguese and their desire to share their food, it also echoes the dictator's emphasis on keeping people within the four walls of their homes and away from civic, collective, or social life. It took many decades for our culture, our city, and our people to recover from this oppression and embrace vibrant café society and street life again, as they had during the blossoming of Lisbon's cafés in the eighteenth century.

Even during these dark times, eating and drinking was still an obsession for the Portuguese. The economic challenges meant that food was scarce for many, particularly in the remote areas of the country, but sometimes difficult situations bring out the best in people; ingredients were eked out and new dishes created. You only have to think of *açorda*, a rich soup made from stale bread and a small amount of fish, seafood, or meat, to realize that there's a "needs must" element that forms the basis of much of our cooking today.

Many *lisboetas* are actually immigrants from elsewhere in Portugal, having left farmland or remote mountain villages to seek a better life in the city. My grandparents came from the Alentejo region in the north and, like many others, they brought recipes with them along with their luggage. They wanted to recreate the specialties of their home region, evoking memories of a different life and place. Each corner of the country has a cooking identity, its own DNA, and Lisbon has become a distillation of all these. It's very much an urban cooking style, a cuisine of "now": fast, sometimes festive, always fun.

Many years ago I left my country in search of a bright future as well as different worlds. At first I thought I would be a marine biologist—in truth, because I couldn't study that subject in Portugal and so would *have* to go abroad to do it. While in Miami, I found my calling; I realized that my passion for food could be translated into a career, and this made me happy. I traveled a fair bit, learning about different tastes, flavors, and cooking methods, and during my journey I worked in some of the very best kitchens. I settled in London and created the restaurants and projects that I am so proud of: Bacchus, Loft Project, Viajante (where I was lucky enough to be awarded a Michelin star), and Chiltern Firehouse. Most recently, I have returned to my roots with the Portuguese restaurant Taberna do Mercado.

Writing this book has meant continuing my culinary journey of discovery, and rooting once again around the Portuguese larder and kitchen. When I smell a simmering *refogado*, the typical Portuguese sauce base, with its aromas of garlic, onion, bay leaf, and paprika, I realize that it's the bedrock of my cooking, a scent that has always been part of my life. Such simplicity sums up the best of Portuguese cooking: taking fantastic produce and letting its own natural flavor be the main player on the plate.

Ours is one of the most overlooked cuisines in Europe, and I believe it's time to truly shout about the food of Portugal. Not only do we stand as tall as our Iberian neighbors in terms of brilliant rice and seafood dishes, but we also braved the unknown seas and brought culinary brilliance from across the continents back to our own kitchens, thus making ours a very distinctive kind of cooking. So, although we have verdant, peppery olive oils and superb tomatoes grown in our own soil, we are also the only country in southern Europe to use fresh cilantro and ground cinnamon liberally in our recipes. Our unique bread-thickened soups, *açordas*, may seem homely but are in fact examples of ingenious adaptation. Our fried snacks can be irresistible—the concept of tempura is owed to the Portuguese. Lastly, we have some of the best sweet treats in the world, and the *pastel de nata* (custard tart), with its yellow filling burnished brown in parts sitting atop a circle of flaky pastry, has achieved a kind of cult status in recent decades.

With our adventurous culinary past and our newfound excitement about the future, Portugal has the potential to be a new force in gastronomy worldwide. We may not have had great finesse in the past, but what we've always had, even during dark times, was some truly wonderful food. Ironically enough, it took leaving home and traveling elsewhere for me to realize that the Portuguese table is one of the best in the world. My cooking now is about reinventing and reimagining the traditional cuisine. We have a phrase in Portuguese that seems to sum it up: *memórias desfocadas* (hazy memories).

The recipes and stories in this book are like the song of the *lisboeta*, and I hope that you'll love them as much as I do.

Cooks' Notes

Portuguese food is essentially simple but, like all cuisines, it has its own peculiarities, beloved ingredients, and distinctive techniques, and there is great variety among the different regions, climates, and terrains. The food of Lisbon is a distillation of all this, since the capital is now home to people who have traveled here from all over the country and our former overseas territories, bringing their much-loved home cooking with them.

Here I explain a few of the more distinctive elements in our cooking, and suggest alternatives for things that may be harder to find. All you really need, though, is good-quality fresh produce.

Ingredients

The area around Lisbon is blessed with one of the greatest natural larders you'll ever come across, from the sardines and mackerel caught by local fishermen and -women and the octopus of Cascais and the red mullet of Setúbal, to the wonderful cilantro, turnip greens, olive oil, and tangy, oozing local cheeses. You may not find exactly the same things where you live, but seek out the best-quality fresh produce you can and adapt where necessary.

Fish and seafood

Portugal is known for the rich variety and pristine quality of its fish and seafood; our marine biodiversity is almost second to none. When developing the recipes for this book, I chose to use the types of fish that are easier to find in other countries, which meant leaving out some of our distinctive seafood dishes. When choosing fish, follow your nose and accept only the very best: look for those that are shimmering and beautiful with firm flesh and only the faintest briny smell. Take advice from your fishmonger and substitute whatever similar, good-quality fish or seafood you can find locally.

Salt cod Salt cod is a national obsession in Portugal, and it has played an important part in our history and culture (see page 4 • 8). However, I prefer to cure my own cod in a salt and sugar mixture (see page 97), which keeps the fish more succulent and helps retain its flavor. If you do use salt cod, it's best to look for a big, fat piece that doesn't seem very dry and make sure you soak it well for at least two or three days in cold water, changing the water every day.

Meat

The Portuguese have a deep-seated love affair with pork. In Lisbon, because we are close to the Alentejo region, where these animals are reared, we adore the delicious nutty flavor of acorn-fed black-foot pig in all its forms, from *presunto* (a delicious cured ham that is easily the equal of Spanish *jamón ibérico* and Italian Parma ham) to simple fried filets and whole legs. We also love to use poultry, game, and young goat (*cabrito*; see page 125). We like to marinate these for a long time, often with wine, garlic, and paprika, so that the flavor really permeates the meat.

Our cured sausages (*enchidos*) are quite brilliant, and once you try them you might be addicted forever. In the past, we would make the best of the produce we had by hanging whatever meat was available over the fireplace to smoke, sometimes for a few days, which would preserve it without the need for refrigeration. Every area of Portugal has its own *enchidos*; my friend Nuno Diniz, who makes a traditional Portuguese stew using as many types as he can find, identified more than one hundred at the last count. *Chouriço* is probably our favorite *enchido*, but we also have *alheira*, a sausage made from meats other than pork, flavored with bread and garlic; *farinheira*, a rich garlic and pork sausage; and linguiça, a soft sausage that is lightly cured and smoked.

Chouriço A smoked sausage flavored with paprika and garlic. I think the best *chouriço* comes from the Alentejo, where it tends to be less heavily smoked and has a subtler flavor. Spanish chorizo, while not identical (it is oilier and has more paprika in it), is similar and can be used as a substitute. (Mexican chorizo, which isn't cured, is not a substitute.)

Morcela A soft sausage made with pigs' blood, this is similar to British black pudding, which can be substituted for *morcela*. Like many recipes that began in country homes, *morcelas* vary, as do the flavorings used; my favorite, and one of the best known, is *morcela da Guarda*.

Pork fat Along with olive oil, pork fat is one of the most used fats in the Portuguese kitchen; it even turns up in desserts and pastries. It is used in a soft form, like lard, or cured until firmer and sliced, a bit like the Italian *lardo di Colonnata*. Jars of spreadable Ibérico pork fat and sliced *lardo* are available in many good supermarkets; butcher-shop lard can also be used.

Cheese and eggs

Every region of Portugal produces its own cheese, and there is a huge array to choose from. Most cheese is made from sheep's milk because cows are more expensive and need more land. Some cheeses can seem quite hard and salty to non-Portuguese tastes, so it's worth finding a good *queijaria* (cheese shop) and tasting before you buy. As well as those listed below, which are used in the recipes, my favorites are *queijo de Azeitão*, a small, soft cheese; *queijo de Nisa*, a semi-hard cheese curdled with thistles; and *queijo Terrincho*, a semi-soft cheese with a distinctive orange crust. Another true gem, served as a snack in many restaurants, is *queijo fresco*, a very fresh cheese no more than twenty-four hours old, made with sweet, fresh cow's milk.

Queijo da Ilha An excellent hard, full-flavored cow's milk cheese from São Jorge in the Azores, which is also known as *queijo São Jorge*. It is often used for grating and cooking; Parmesan or pecorino make good substitutes.

Queijo da Serra This is a very special cheese from Covilhã, near Serra da Estrela, the highest mountain in Portugal, where the long-horned sheep whose milk is used to make the cheese are pastured on lush green slopes. It's sold at different stages of maturity; the most prized version is the very soft, ripe one found in winter and spring, which we serve by removing the crust and spooning out the middle. It is full-flavored, even pungent, depending on its age.

Eggs Eggs are one of the most important ingredients in Portuguese cuisine, particularly in desserts. Traditionally, egg whites were used in convents to starch clerical gowns and to clarify wine, and the leftover egg yolks were used to create an incredible repertoire of desserts (*doces conventuais*), with the addition of sugar and, in many cases, cinnamon. In the recipes here, all eggs should be large size and free range.

Legumes, vegetables, and fruits

Portuguese terrain is very fertile, with fabulous growing conditions, so you might find it surprising that fruit and vegetables are not a bigger feature of our cuisine. We do grow wonderful produce, though, and in Lisbon even the tiniest corner shop has lush cilantro, flavorful tomatoes, juicy oranges, and verdant olives. Beans and legumes are grown and eaten all over the country, the most common varieties being chickpeas, white beans, red kidney beans, and black-eyed peas, which are used in soups and stews such as *feijoada* (page 138).

Cabbage *Couve galega*, a dark-leaved brassica similar to collard greens, is our favorite type of cabbage and features in what is commonly regarded as Portugal's national dish, *caldo verde* (page 89). Kale, collards, Swiss chard, and Savoy cabbage can all be substituted for *couve galega*, depending on the dish.

Chickpeas These are a staple of Portuguese cooking, and in Lisbon we treasure a dish called *meia desfeita* (page 103), in which they are cooked until

fat and tender along with cod and served with lemon, eggs, and cilantro. They
are also used to make delicious purées with tomatoes, garlic, and a good
measure of olive oil.

Onions These are pretty much the backbone of Portuguese cooking, a
particular favorite being the large white ones. You can use ordinary yellow
onions here unless the recipe specifies otherwise.

Oranges Orange trees are abundant all over southern Portugal, and in parts
of Lisbon you'll see them growing in backyards. They're used in many dishes,
the juice often lending its perfume and acidity to marinades and dressings.
Note that in the recipes that follow, all citrus fruit should be unwaxed.

Potatoes Since they arrived in Portugal during the Discoveries, potatoes
have featured in most meals. Strangely, we often serve them with rice, which
to me is a bit of a carbohydrate overload. Portuguese potatoes, yellow and
earthy, come into their own in the many dishes that use salt cod, where the
two elements offset each other gloriously. Yukon golds can be used instead.

Turnip greens Along with cabbage, turnip greens (*grelos*) are one of the
few green vegetables that we Portuguese crave. They are typically boiled, or
fried with garlic and lots of olive oil, and make a wonderful side dish. Other
dark leafy brassicas could be substituted.

Herbs, spices, and pantry staples

One of the most distinctive features of Portuguese cooking is its use of
flavorings, which is quite unlike the other southern European cuisines in
its use of cilantro, chile, orange, and cinnamon—although we do share
the Mediterranean love of good olive oil. Sauces, marinades, and dressings
like *piso* (page 98), piri piri oil (page 156), and *massa de pimentão* (red
pepper paste; page 173) are used liberally to add layers of flavor.

Aguardente velha *Aguardente* is the national Portuguese liquor or
"firewater," which comes in many varieties. *Aguardente velha* is distilled
from wine and aged in port barrels; its closest substitute is brandy.

Bay leaves Bay is a consistent undertone in Portuguese cooking. I like
to use fresh leaves for their aromatic pungency, but feel free to substitute dried
bay leaves.

Bread Being at its heart a thrifty cuisine, the Portuguese culinary repertoire
includes countless uses for bread, a staple of the national diet for centuries.

It's an essential ingredient, for example, in *migas* and *açordas*. One of the best-known types is *broa* (page 299), a rustic bread made partly with cornmeal and traditionally baked in large loaves in wood-fired ovens. Its dense yellow crumb is almost cakelike, which helps it age well. Although they are quite different in taste and texture, sourdough or a good-quality rustic loaf such as *pain de campagne* could be used instead in many of the recipes here.

Cilantro Cilantro's distinctive taste defines many of the flavors we identify as Portuguese, most noticeably when it is combined with garlic, lemon, and olive oil in the herb sauce *piso* (page 98).

Cinnamon Ever since it was first brought to our shores from India, cinnamon has been adored in Portugal. It is used liberally with sugar and egg yolks in our desserts and cakes. You will also find it, perhaps surprisingly, in some of our savory dishes.

Mustard We love to serve sweet mustard with snacks and sandwiches. The local brand is Savora, but any sweet mustard, such as French's, will do.

Olive oil Olive oil is one of Portugal's great treasures and is used throughout our cooking—not least because many people have olive trees and make their own. It really does vary throughout the country depending on which olive varietal of the many dozens cultivated has been used, and flavor profiles range from grassy and bitter to nutty and sweet. I always like to use a good-quality olive oil, and finish off many dishes with a generous swirl of extra-virgin oil.

Paprika This is used liberally for its smoky intensity, piquancy, and beautiful color. Portuguese paprika (*colorau*) can be substituted with Spanish sweet smoked paprika.

Piri piri The piri piri is a fiery chile pepper that was brought to our shores from Africa. We love to use it in both fresh and dried form, and homemade piri piri oil (page 156) is a staple on dining tables all around the country.

Rice This is extremely important in Portuguese cooking and agriculture, and our *arroz* dishes (pages 199 and 217) easily rival the paellas and risottos of Spain and Italy. Both short- and long-grain varieties are grown here, but it's the short-grain Carolino rice that I like best. If you have trouble finding it, white Japanese sushi rice or Spanish Bomba rice are good alternatives. We like our rice dishes to be served *malandrinho*, quite loose and runny in texture.

Techniques

Although we Portuguese have our own distinctive preparations, such as our way of cooking *arroz* (rice dishes), and *migas* and *açordas* (bread-thickened soups and stews), no special techniques are needed. Here I have explained some of the ways I like to cook, which are all about maximizing freshness and flavor.

Preparing vegetables Whenever possible, I peel and cut vegetables, especially onions and fennel, just before I cook them to help keep them fresh. I also like to remove the green germ from the center of garlic cloves, which can taste bitter, before crushing them. Note that all vegetables in the recipes are medium size, unless otherwise specified.

Seasoning Thanks to Portugal's long coastline we have many salt beds, and salt has played an important part in our history over many centuries. In cooking we use coarse sea salt and fine table salt and add it liberally but, of course, the amount you use is up to you. I like to add a little seasoning at every stage of cooking a dish, and then just sprinkle over a little flaky salt such as *fleur de sel* or Maldon salt at the end. I use ground white pepper, rather than black, for most of my dishes. Along with salt and pepper, freshly squeezed lemon juice and paprika are the other key elements of seasoning.

Deep-frying In Portugal we really love to deep-fry our food; our passion for crunchy little tidbits knows no bounds. Do take care when deep-frying; do not overfill the pan with oil and never leave it unattended. Fry in small batches and eat as soon as possible after frying.

Quick cooking Many of the recipes in this book, such as Café-Style Steak (page 126), Garlic and Chile Squid with Green Beans (page 177), and Quick-Fried Beef with Pickles (page 188), can be cooked very quickly. For dishes like these, the instructions are really more of a guide. It's best to read the recipe in full first to make sure all is clear, then put the book down and cook it quickly from start to finish.

Oven temperatures In Portugal we often cook at high temperatures. In particular we like our pastries baked quite dark, ideally with heat from both the top and the bottom of the oven. This effect can be recreated at home by using a higher oven temperature than you might be used to; start by following the temperature given in the recipe, check the dish regularly, and increase or reduce the temperature if necessary.

Pas

téis

In Lisbon, every day has a kind of eating rhythm. *Pastéis* (pastries) are taken in the morning; a person might have a piece of toast at home, but they soon crave the outdoors and head down to their local *pastelaria* for *uma bica*, an espresso-sized coffee, and a *pastel* (one pastry is a *pastel*; *pastéis* means at least two).

In Lisbon there is a *pastelaria* serving cakes and pastries on every other corner. Look for the words *fabrico proprio* when you choose one, as it means "produced by us," and the baked goods will be made especially for this place, and possibly one or two other establishments. I once sneaked in through the back door of a *pastelaria* at around 10 o'clock at night just to breathe in the dense, sweet aroma and watch the masters of cake at work. It was quite enthralling to see them stacking up trays of *bolos de arroz* (soft rice cakes) and set about baking their next batch of *pão de deus* (bread of God) for the day ahead.

The *pastel de nata*, or Custard Tart (page 33), is our most famous pastry, a global export eaten in cafés around the world. But it's just one among hundreds of *pastéis* made in Portugal, a country in which the day is not complete without something sweet and baked. Homemade *pastéis* really are perfect for a lovely morning treat on the weekend but, of course, you can eat them any time of the day.

Historically, it was only the very wealthy and the church who could afford to buy sugar imported from Portugal's colonies. Convents and monasteries became centers of production for cakes and sweets, or *doce*, supplementing their income with the sale of baked treasures. The nuns who invented some of the *pastéis* recipes clearly liked to have a little fun, christening their creations *papos de anjo* (angels' double chins) and *barriga de freiras* (nuns' bellies). Others must have had a poetic bent, coming up with names like *sonhos* (dreams), *suspiros* (sighs), and *travesseiros* (pillows).

Many of these pastries included a combination of sugar and egg yolks, to make the most of the yolks that were left over when the whites of eggs were used to starch vestments and clarify convent-produced wine. Adding the flavors of the oranges, almonds, and cinnamon that had originally been introduced by the Moors, Portuguese pastry makers conjured up some of the sweetest, richest confections in the world.

One of my absolute favorite pastries is the *jesuita* (page 28), which is cone-shaped, like the hats worn by members of the Jesuit order. The recipe dates back more than a hundred years and it can vary depending on the *pastelaria*; the base is always made from buttery puff pastry, and the *jesuitas* are filled with *doce de ovos*, or sweet egg cream. Variations include hard-laminated royal icing set to a crisp or, better to my taste, a light sugary glaze and a topping of toasted almond nibs or flakes.

I have chosen my most cherished *pastéis* for the following chapter: the ones I would stand in line for or get up early to make, just so I could eat them warm with a *bica* in the morning. Almost every pastry is wrapped up in a memory for me—like Proust's madeleines, only a little bit eggier.

Almond cream triangles
Jesuitas

Makes 6

⅞ cup/200 ml sugar syrup (page 33)
6 egg yolks
Finely grated zest of 1 lemon
1¾ ounces/50 g ground almonds
2 (11-ounce/320 g) sheets all-butter
    puff pastry
1 egg, beaten lightly with a dash of water
1½ ounces/40 g sliced almonds

This is one of my most beloved *pastéis*: a triangle of pastry named after the Jesuit monk's hat it resembles. Different versions have developed over the last hundred years; in my favorite type, the dough is baked dark and crispy, the almonds are toasted, and the pastries are stuffed with almond egg cream. I love to buy a couple and eat them on a bench at Praça Luís de Camões, a central square that is fabulous for watching the world go by while savoring my *jesuitas*.

Preheat the oven to 430°F/220°C (convection 390°F/200°C) and line a baking sheet with baking parchment.

Heat the sugar syrup in a pan until just boiling, then leave to cool for a few minutes. Whisk the yolks lightly in a heatproof bowl, then pour the sugar syrup over the yolks, whisking all the time. Pour the mixture back into the pan and cook gently over low heat for 10 to 12 minutes, or until thickened, stirring constantly. Remove from the heat and stir in the lemon zest and ground almonds. Pour it out onto a plate to cool, covered with plastic wrap to prevent a skin from forming.

Make sure the pastry is in two large rectangles about ⅛ inch/ 3 mm thick, rolling them out a little if necessary. Cut each one into 6 large triangles. Spread half of the triangles with 1 tablespoon of the almond egg cream. Place the remaining triangles on top and gently press the edges to seal. Lightly brush the tops with the beaten egg and sprinkle the sliced almonds on top. Place them on the prepared baking sheet and chill for 10 minutes. Bake for 20 minutes, or until golden brown and cooked through. Leave to cool on a wire rack before serving.

Almond and butternut tarts
Tartes de amêndoa e abóbora

Makes 4

For the filling

3 ounces/80 g butternut squash, peeled
   and cut into small pieces

1 tablespoon olive oil

7 tablespoons/90 g superfine sugar,
   plus 1 teaspoon

A pinch of smoked paprika

6½ tablespoons/90 g butter, softened,
   plus extra for greasing

2 eggs

4 ounces/125 g ground almonds

3 tablespoons/30 g all-purpose flour

Finely grated zest of 1 orange

For the topping

5 tablespoons/70 g butter

6 tablespoons/75 g superfine sugar

5 ounces/150 g sliced almonds

5 teaspoons/25 ml whole milk

Confectioners' sugar, for dusting

Early one morning, after antique hunting at the Feira da Ladra flea market, I stopped at a café for a coffee and had the perfect almond tart. The nuts were crisp and the filling was crumbly and buttery, flavored with almond and orange. As I sat there in the sunshine I promised myself I'd make my own version as a tribute to that moment.

Preheat the oven to 430°F/220°C (convection 390°F/200°C) and grease four 5-inch/13-cm tart tins with butter.

To make the filling — Put the butternut squash on a baking sheet and toss with the olive oil, the 1 teaspoon of sugar, and the paprika. Roast for 30 minutes, or until soft and caramelized. Purée with an immersion blender until smooth.

Cream the butter and the remaining 7 tablespoons/90 g of sugar until light and fluffy. Add the eggs one by one. Stir in the ground almonds. Fold in the flour, then the butternut squash purée and the orange zest. Divide the mixture evenly among the tins and bake for 10 minutes, or until just set.

To make the topping — Melt the butter and sugar in a small pan over low heat. When the sugar has dissolved, stir in the almonds and milk and cook for a few minutes, stirring constantly. Divide the topping among the tarts and bake for 4 more minutes.

I like to dust the tarts lightly with confectioners' sugar when they come out of the oven. Leave them to cool for a few minutes before taking them out of the tins; the topping will firm as it cools.

Custard tarts
Pastéis de nata

Makes 6

Melted butter, for greasing
1 (11-ounce/320 g) sheet all-butter
    puff pastry

For the custard
1 cup/250 ml whole milk
1 cinnamon stick
A few strips of lemon zest
4 teaspoons/20 g butter
2 tablespoons all-purpose flour
1 teaspoon cornstarch
2 egg yolks

For the sugar syrup
1 cup plus 2 tablespoons/
    225 g superfine sugar
1 cinnamon stick
A few strips of lemon zest

Sugar and ground cinnamon, for dusting

When you mention Portuguese food, most people think of *pastéis de nata*, our glorious custard tarts. They became popular in the mid-nineteenth century when monks at the Mosteiro dos Jerónimos in Belém began selling them to help make a living. When I was a child, my grandmother would take me to Pastéis de Belém, where the original versions are still sold. I'd swipe her coffee spoon when she wasn't looking and scoop out all the custard before eating the crust. The filling here has a soft scent of citrus and should be really runny—just perfect for small boys with coffee spoons.

Brush 6 individual muffin tins generously with melted butter, then chill them in the fridge. (If you don't have individual tins, use half of a 12-hole muffin tin.)

Make sure the pastry is in a large ⅛-inch/2 to 3 mm-thick rectangle, rolling it out a little if necessary, then roll it up lengthwise into a tight sausage shape about 2 inches/5 cm in diameter. Slice this into 6 discs ½ to ¾ inch/1 to 2 cm thick (any leftover pastry can be frozen to use another day). Press the discs into the tins with your fingers, stretching or rolling them out to fit, making sure they come to just below the tops of the tins. Chill them while you make the custard.

To make the custard — Heat ⅔ cup/150 ml of the milk in a pan over medium heat with the cinnamon, lemon zest, and 2 teaspoons/10 g of the butter, bringing it to just below the boiling point. Remove it from the heat and leave it to infuse for 10 minutes.

Remove the cinnamon and lemon zest. In a bowl, mix the flour and cornstarch to a thin paste with the remaining ⅓ cup/100 ml milk, adding the milk gradually to prevent lumps. Pour the warm infused milk over the paste, stirring well, then pour the mixture back into the pan. Cook, stirring gently, over low heat for a few minutes, or until it thickens to a heavy cream consistency. Whisk in the remaining 2 teaspoons/10 g butter and remove from the heat. →

→ *To make the sugar syrup* — Put the ingredients in a pan with 5 tablespoons/75 ml of water and cook over medium heat for 5 minutes, until the sugar dissolves. Cook over low heat until you have a light brown, fragrant caramel, swirling the pan occasionally.

Carefully add 5 tablespoons/75 ml more water and return the pan to a gentle heat to dissolve any solid caramel, then strain it into a heatproof bowl. Pour half the syrup into the custard and whisk well. (The leftover syrup will keep in the fridge in an airtight container for 4 weeks, and can be used to make the egg cream on page 28.)

Preheat the oven to its highest setting and put a baking sheet on the top shelf. Just before cooking the tarts, pour the custard into a glass measuring cup and stir in the egg yolks. Add a splash of milk to bring the quantity up to 1¼ cups/300 ml, if necessary. Pour the custard into the pastry-lined muffin tins and bake on the hot baking sheet for 9 to 13 minutes, or until the tops are quite dark, rotating them if necessary to make sure they color evenly.

Brush the tarts with a little of the remaining sugar syrup, then leave to cool slightly in the tins before removing and cooling on a wire rack. The custard will continue to set as it cools but should still be creamy and quite soft in the center. Sprinkle with sugar and cinnamon just before serving, as we do in Portugal.

Carrot "cheese" cakes
Queijadas de cenoura

Makes 12

1½ pounds/660 g carrots, peeled
5 tablespoons/70 g butter, softened,
    plus a little extra for greasing
1¼ cups/250 g superfine sugar
4 eggs
¾ cup/100 g all-purpose flour
A pinch of fine sea salt
Finely grated zest of 1 lemon
Finely grated zest of 1 orange

Queijada literally means something made with *queijo* (cheese)—in this case, small cheesecakes. The *queijadas* from the town of Sintra are especially famous; my grandfather and I used to drive up to the mountains in his Citroën DS just to get a packet of them. This version was created by Diana Neto, our pastry chef at Taberna do Mercado and, ironically, the cheese has been omitted to give a lighter texture, while carrot has been added for flavor and substance.

Preheat the oven to 430°F/220°C (convection 390°F/200°C) and grease a nonstick 12-hole muffin tin with butter. Chop 1 pound/500 g of the carrots and coarsely grate the rest. Bring a pan of salted water to a boil and cook the chopped carrots until soft. Drain, then blend until smooth with an immersion blender. Set aside to cool.

In a large bowl, cream the butter and sugar until pale and fluffy. Fold in the puréed carrots until well combined. Add the eggs one by one and mix until smooth. Gently fold in the flour, salt, grated carrots, and lemon and orange zests. Fill each muffin hole with 3 tablespoons of batter. Gently pat the surface smooth with the back of a wet spoon. Bake for 25 minutes, or until a skewer comes out clean. Cool on a wire rack before serving.

Classic palmiers
Palmiers

Makes 12 to 15

1 cup/200 g superfine sugar
2 strips lemon zest
2 strips orange zest
1 cinnamon stick
1 vanilla pod, split lengthwise
3 (11-ounce/320 g) sheets all-butter
    puff pastry
Granulated sugar, for sprinkling
Ground cinnamon, for sprinkling (optional)

Palmiers are not Portuguese in origin—they're French, and the word literally means "palm tree"—but we love them. In Lisbon the *pastelarias* sell several variations: *cobertos*, which are covered with a sugary glaze; *miniaturas*, which are small in size; and my favorite, *recheados*, in which two pieces are sandwiched together with several different fillings. I have given the simple, classic version here, but you could also try sandwiching them with the sweet potato custard, opposite, or the filling for the *jesuitas* on page 28.

Start by making a sugar syrup: put the sugar, citrus zests, cinnamon stick, and vanilla pod in a pan with ⅞ cup/200 ml of water. Cook over low heat until the sugar has dissolved, then boil for 2 minutes. Strain.

Make sure the pastry is in three large rectangles about ⅛ inch/ 3 mm thick, rolling them out a little if necessary. Sprinkle a clean surface generously with granulated sugar, place a sheet of pastry on top, and sprinkle it evenly with sugar. Roll lightly with a rolling pin to seal the layers. Place the next sheet on top and sprinkle with more sugar. Repeat with the third sheet. Roll out the three sheets lightly into a layered rectangle. With a short end nearest you, fold the top third of the pastry down toward you and fold the bottom third up away from you to cover the top third, a bit like folding a letter in three. Roll the pastry out again to roughly the same size as the original sheet. Starting from one of the long edges, roll the pastry up tightly to the center, stopping halfway. Roll up the other side to meet it, then wrap the pastry in plastic wrap and chill it for 1 hour.

Line a baking sheet with baking parchment. Using a sharp knife, cut the pastry roll widthwise into slices about 1¼ inches/ 3 cm thick. Line them up on the prepared baking sheet and chill for 20 minutes. Preheat the oven to 430°F/220°C (convection 390°F/200°C).

Bake on the top shelf for 12 to 15 minutes, turning halfway through cooking so they color evenly. As soon as they come out of the oven, brush them with the sugar syrup and sprinkle with cinnamon. Cool on a wire rack before serving.

Doughnuts with sweet potato custard *Sonhos com creme de batata doce*

Makes around 20

14 ounces/400 g sweet potatoes

For the dough
1 cup/250 ml whole milk
¾ cup plus 2 tablespoons/200 g butter
2 cups plus 2 tablespoons/300 g
    all-purpose flour
A pinch of fine sea salt
5 eggs

For the sweet potato custard
2 egg yolks
5 tablespoons/50 g all-purpose flour
2 cups/500 ml whole milk
½ cup/100 g superfine sugar
1 vanilla pod, split lengthwise
1 cinnamon stick
Finely grated zest of 1 orange

Vegetable oil, for frying
Superfine sugar, for dusting

Sonhos means "dreams" in Portuguese, probably thanks to the lightness of the doughnuts or the fact that once you eat one, you will keep dreaming about it. In Lisbon they are usually eaten around Christmastime, but I make them whenever I feel like it. Some traditional recipes for sonhos include pumpkin or sweet potato, used here in the custard. My sonhos are lighter and slightly less sweet than the ones you'll find in Portugal.

Preheat the oven to 390°F/200°C (convection 355°F/180°C). Put the sweet potatoes on a baking sheet and roast for 45 minutes, or until cooked through. Leave to cool slightly, then peel and purée with an immersion blender until smooth.

To make the dough — Heat the milk, 1 cup/250 ml of water, and the butter in a pan over medium heat. Sift the flour onto a sheet of baking parchment. When the butter has melted, tip in the flour all at once, using the baking parchment as a chute. Beat with a spatula until the dough comes away from the side of the pan. Remove from the heat and keep beating until the dough has cooled and thickened. Add about ⅔ cup/160 g of the sweet potato purée and the salt and stir well. Beat in the eggs one by one, making sure that each one is fully incorporated before adding the next, until the dough is smooth and glossy. You may not need to add all the eggs. Transfer to a bowl, cover, and refrigerate for 30 minutes.

To make the sweet potato custard — Whisk the egg yolks and flour in a bowl. Heat the rest of the ingredients with about ¾ cup/200 g of the sweet potato purée in a pan over medium heat, whisking well. Gradually pour the hot mixture over the yolks. Strain it back into the pan and cook for about 6 minutes over low heat, stirring continuously, until thickened.

To fry the doughnuts, fill a large, heavy-bottomed pan one-third full with oil and heat until it reaches 355°F/180°C (or until a cube of bread sizzles and turns golden brown almost immediately). Using 2 tablespoons, spoon the dough into the pan in small batches, frying for a few minutes, turning as needed, until golden brown. Remove and drain on paper towels. Roll the doughnuts in superfine sugar while still warm. Serve with the custard on the side for dipping.

Custard-filled doughnuts
Bolas de Berlim

Makes about 12

3 eggs
Finely grated zest of 2 oranges
3½ cups/500 g all-purpose flour
⅔ cup/130 g superfine sugar
1 teaspoon fine sea salt
¾ ounce/25 g fresh yeast, or
⅜ ounce/12 g active dry yeast
½ cup/110 g butter, cut into cubes
and softened

For the egg cream filling
⅞ cup/200 ml sugar syrup (page 33)
6 egg yolks
Finely grated zest of 1 lemon
1⅓ ounces/40 g ground almonds

Vegetable oil, for frying
Superfine sugar, for dusting

Bolas de Berlim **literally means "balls from Berlin," and these were first brought to Portugal by Jewish refugees. We had to make them our own, of course, so some crafty genius decided to slit the doughnut open and fill it with egg custard. I love the yeasty flavor of the soft dough, the sugary crust, and the creamy filling. Get creative when you make these yourself: you can use plain old jam, Nutella, or whipped cream as a filling—or you could even create a savory doughnut like my favorite, crab and crème fraîche, using exactly the same dough recipe.**

Mix the eggs, ½ cup/130 ml of water, and the orange zest in a bowl and refrigerate for 2 hours before using.

Combine the flour, sugar, and salt in the bowl of a stand mixer using the paddle attachment. Whisk the yeast into the egg and water mixture, pour it into the mixer bowl, and then mix for 20 minutes, or until the dough is smooth and comes away from the sides of the bowl. Add the butter gradually, mixing until it is fully incorporated and the dough is smooth and stretchy. Put the dough in a lightly oiled bowl, cover it loosely with plastic wrap, and leave it in the fridge to rise overnight.

To make the filling — Heat the sugar syrup in a pan until it is just boiling, then leave to cool for a few minutes. Whisk the egg yolks lightly in a heatpoof bowl, then pour the sugar syrup over them, whisking constantly. Pour the mixture back into the pan and cook gently over low heat for 10 to 12 minutes, or until thickened, stirring constantly. Remove from the heat and stir in the lemon zest and ground almonds. Pour onto a plate and leave to cool to room temperature, covered with plastic wrap to prevent a skin from forming.

To shape the doughnuts, divide the dough into 12 roughly 1½-ounce/40 g pieces and shape each piece into a small ball with your hands. Cover them with a tea towel and leave to rise for 30 minutes, or until doubled in size.

Fill a large, heavy-bottomed pan one-third full with oil and heat it to 355°F/180°C, or until a cube of bread sizzles and turns golden brown almost immediately. Fry the doughnuts in batches for about 2 minutes, or until golden brown. Remove, drain on paper towels, and roll in superfine sugar while warm, then leave them to cool.

Make a slit in the middle of each doughnut without cutting all the way through. Spoon the egg cream filling inside and serve immediately.

Almond pillows
Travesseiros

Makes 4

7 tablespoons/100 ml sugar syrup (page 33)
3 egg yolks
Finely grated zest of 1 lemon
2 ounces/60 g ground almonds
1 (11-ounce/320 g) sheet all-butter
    puff pastry
1 egg, lightly beaten with a little water
Superfine sugar, for sprinkling

These delicate pastries look a bit like pillows (hence the name), and are filled with almond egg cream. Like *queijadas*, they come from Sintra, onetime summer home of monarchs and nobility and now a busy UNESCO World Heritage Site. I used to love wandering off the beaten track there with my beloved grandmother Albertina, finding nooks and crannies of peace and serenity. Our path led to a *pastelaria* that was home to the best *travesseiros* I've ever come across. Albertina has passed away now but when I make *travesseiros* I think of her and taste tender memories.

Heat the sugar syrup in a pan until it is just boiling, then leave it to cool for a few minutes. Whisk the egg yolks lightly in a heatproof bowl, then pour the sugar syrup over them, whisking constantly. Pour the mixture back into the pan and cook gently over low heat for 10 to 12 minutes, or until thickened, stirring constantly. Remove from the heat and stir in the lemon zest and ground almonds. Pour into a shallow bowl and leave to cool to room temperature.

Line a baking sheet with baking parchment. Roll out the pastry to ⅛ inch/3 mm thick and cut it into 4 rectangular strips about 3 inches/8 to 9 cm wide. Put a heaping tablespoon of the filling in the middle of each rectangle and brush around the edge lightly with the beaten egg. Fold the top half of the pastry over the filling to form a pillow. Lightly press the sides to seal the pastry. Put the pillows on the baking sheet and chill for 15 minutes. Preheat the oven to 430°F/220°C (convection 390°F/200°C).

Bake for 20 minutes, or until the pastry is cooked through. Sprinkle with sugar and serve the little pillows warm.

Discoveries

I'm standing at a stall in the bustling
vegetable market at Lisbon's Mercado
da Ribeira where piri piri chiles
are hanging in bunches, their bright
red color warning of the fire within.
Looking at these essential ingredients
in Portuguese cooking, I find myself
reflecting on how they first came to
our larders. Along with black pepper,
cinnamon, cloves, ginger, and nutmeg,
piri piri became popular in the sixteenth century, when Portuguese navigators brought them home from their
ocean adventures. It was a period known
as the Age of Discovery, and indeed
the New World offered plants and vegetables that would change the European
diet forever when they first arrived
here: tomatoes, potatoes, corn, peppers, peanuts, and exotic fruits that
turned our taste buds upside down.

From the market, I walk along nearby
Rua do Arsenal and step into one of
the little old-fashioned grocery shops
there, a *mercearia* in which cloth
sacks are filled with dozens of different beans and legumes that originated in South and Central America and
Africa. All kinds of new beans began
to fill Portuguese shelves during the
sixteenth century because they were
easily transportable when dried and a
great source of protein, filling, and
cheap—and to this day they are a main-
stay of our cooking. There are also
giant bags of short- and long-grain
rice. Seeing them like this makes me
think of how rice was introduced to the
Iberian peninsula in the eighth century by the Moors, when it was a rarity
only really enjoyed by the rich. It was
not until the Discoveries, when vast
quantities of rice came back from Asia,

that it became a staple, because it was easily cultivated in lagoon paddies in central and southern Portugal. Lining the shelves are other goods brought to us during this amazing period: coffee, tea, chocolate, and probably the biggest food import of all—sugar.

When the Moors first invaded Portugal they brought with them almonds, citrus fruits, figs, and a cooking pot known as a *cataplana* (a shell-shaped vessel of two halves that clip together, which acts like a kind of pressure cooker). I imagine that our taste for spices began with the Moors, but it wasn't until they were made more affordable by the Atlantic sea missions that they became key ingredients in Portuguese cuisine.

Portugal's overseas conquests began in 1415 when Prince Henry the Navigator became fascinated with the idea of exploring the coast of Africa. He dispatched his galleons on incredible voyages, and within five years the beautiful, verdant island of Madeira was found. With Henry's nephew, King John II, the era known as the Age of Discovery really began, along with Portugal's dominance of global trade routes. John created a Council of Scholars to help draw up plans for Portugal to find new territories across the seas, and promoted a campaign of misinformation to throw competing foreign adventurers off track. Lisbon was teeming with spies desperate to learn details of sea routes, or maybe catch sight of Portugal's new maps. Stories of dragons and unicorns and man-eating snakes abounded, all of it fantastical propaganda that

wouldn't be out of place in the storybooks I read to my kids.

As more new lands were discovered, great treasures were brought back to Lisbon and it soon became the richest city in Europe, if not the world. It was abuzz with investors, missionaries, and mercenaries, all focused on the trade flowing in along the River Tejo, which allowed ships to dock just a few miles from the heart of town. The influences of the New World adventures could be seen everywhere: in cooking, in architecture, and in the faces of the people who came to live there.

The ambition to expand territory across the sea was insatiable, motivated first by geography—with its back to Spain, Portugal had nowhere else to go but out into the Atlantic—and second by the fact that the country was almost bankrupt. Opening the seas would allow the pursuit of gold and incredibly lucrative spices. European cooks enjoyed the exotic flavors that were now increasingly available, as well as the opportunity to show off wealth and status by using them—at the time, some spices were worth thousands of times more than in the places where they had been grown. For years Venice was the very center of Europe's spice market, but if Lisbon could take its place, the treasury would surely spill over. And it did. The story goes that when the Portuguese explorer Vasco da Gama opened up the sea route to India in 1498, a single ship loaded with cinnamon was valuable enough to cover the whole cost of his expedition. In the end, Portugal became wealthier than anyone could ever have imagined and headed up an empire spanning four continents. It was the country that gave rise to modern globalization, linking Europe with Asia and the rest of the world through trade routes to West Africa, India, China, Brazil, and Japan. By the sixteenth century, Portugal had the largest high-seas fleet in Europe.

These seafaring exploits were a two-way passage in culinary terms. We took our recipes overseas—our *refogado* stew base forms the backbone of the cuisine in Portuguese-speaking countries such as Brazil and Angola—but we brought back theirs too. One of my favorite things, our spicy *chamuças*, are a perfect example of a culinary hybrid, a rich legacy of the Portuguese introduction of savory *pastéis* to India, where spices were added to create the triangular samosas that are now almost universal. Goanese *vindalho* (vindaloo) comes from our *vinha d'*alhos, a wine and garlic marinade, with the wine replaced by vinegar, which is more readily available in India. The Alphonso mangoes grown in western India are named after Afonso de Albuquerque, the naval commander who established Portuguese colonies there; because of his explorers' green-fingered grafting skills, the world's sweetest mango was born. Back in Portugal, we developed recipes that included these previously unknown ingredients—a perfect example is piri piri sauce, made fiery with chiles from Angola and Mozambique.

In pursuit of spices, the Portuguese set out to control trade in the Moluccas in Indonesia, now known as the Maluku archipelago, and once simply dubbed the Spice Islands because they were the world's biggest source of high-quality nutmeg, mace, and cloves. We ruled Sri Lanka, then called Ceylon, for more than a century, and this was the main source of the best cinnamon, without a doubt our country's favorite spice. Although we have pursued seasonings in many corners of the world, we actually use them very sparingly in the kitchen. You'll find that it's only cinnamon (*canela*) that is scattered prodigiously in Portuguese cooking and that other aromatics are added lightly, giving just a subtle hint of flavor to a dish.

The thing that made the Discoveries possible was the caravel, a ship that used a different design from the galleons previously deployed on the high seas. Powered by sails rather than oarsmen, these new vessels required a smaller crew, and their food supplies would stretch further, meaning they could spend more time at sea. Able to sail windward, caravels were fast and agile, just like the new nautical technology on board: the astrolabe, the compass, and the Portolan chart. They were remarkable ships.

In modern Portugal you don't have to look very far to find traces of this past. Our obsession with coffee comes from the Discoveries, of course, when we realized that the coffee beans of Ethiopia would also grow fantastically well in the Portuguese colonies of Angola, Brazil, East Timor, and São Tomé and Príncipe. On a recent visit to one of Europe's last remaining wood-fired coffee roasteries, Flor da Selva

in Lisbon's traditional Madragoa neighborhood, I noticed that all the burlap sacks are printed with the names of these countries, where the beans inside are still grown. Every time I think of the Discoveries and those brave adventurers heading out across the ocean it blows my mind. But there's no denying that conquering other nations involved murder, brutality, and astonishing inhumanity, and I can't help but feel deep shame that Portugal played such an enormous part in this. We were the first nation to engage in the Atlantic slave trade, tearing men and women from Africa and shipping them to the New World, where they were treated barbarically. The Portuguese built the first slave fort, Elmina Castle, on the coast of what is now Ghana. By the seventeenth century, Portugal was the major trader in African slaves, supplying not only their own colonies, but the Spanish too. Slavery was abolished in Portugal in 1761 and across the empire in 1836, but many Portuguese people continued the trade for decades.

I feel torn when I think of the Portuguese-speaking countries around the world, like Brazil, Macau, and Angola, because I know that before the caravels arrived, the people there spoke another language. And yet I also find it remarkable that a small nation like Portugal could have such a huge impact on the world, bringing so many edible treasures back home to become part of Europe's culinary landscape.

I find it hard to imagine what life looked like during the Discoveries, so I sometimes go to the Museu Nacional de Arte Antiga in the Lapa area of Lisbon. I head upstairs and, among the cases filled with bounty brought back by Portuguese navigators, seek out four gloriously decorated panels known as the Namban Folding Screens. These depict the arrival of the Portuguese in the port of Nagasaki in the sixteenth century. I like to study the faces and costumes of the Europeans, called "southern barbarians" by the Japanese, with their exaggerated features and clothes, large noses and mustaches, and voluminous pantaloons; things the Japanese people had never seen before. There's a festive atmosphere as the opulent cargo is unloaded on shore: people ride on elephants and are carried in palanquins; there are Jesuit missionaries and merchants and explorers. I like to imagine the feast that might unfold, at which the food of Portugal is about to meet that of Japan—two cuisines I adore.

At other times I walk along the Tejo at sunset to watch the dying light hit the rose-tinted stone of the Padrão dos Descobrimentos, a statue in the shape of the prow of a caravel that celebrates the Discoveries. Henry the Navigator is to the front, and sixteen other figures—missionaries, scientists, artists, cartographers, and explorers— are gathered behind him. And although this 184-foot-high structure (built during the Salazar dictatorship) exudes nationalism, it does make me marvel at what these men did, as I stand here at the very point where Portuguese ships began their journeys across the Atlantic. They changed the world forever, and brought it to our doorstep.

Salg

ados

Salgados are snacks or savories: little finger foods that you can eat in just a couple of bites. Unlike *petiscos*, which we tend to eat later in the day, these are enjoyed from the late morning onward in cafés, *tascas* (small restaurants), snack bars, and many *pastelarias*. We generally eat them at around 11 o'clock or midday, because this is when they're freshest. You can stand at the counter and have a plate of *salgados* and a *lambreta* (a tiny glass of cold beer) in just a couple of minutes. Sometimes, with an admirable lack of ceremony, you won't even get a plate, just a paper napkin.

The vast majority of *salgados* are fried and I like to eat them straight from the pan, when they're all crispy on the outside and soft on the inside. I hate cold *salgados* but, sadly, this is mostly how they're sold. In Lisbon, it's really worth getting a recommendation for a place that sends them out from the kitchen in small batches at regular intervals. Walk straight past *salgados* that have been left to die in the window, or the ones on the counter with a pool of oil around them, or those that just look a bit floppy.

Portugal's most popular *salgado* is without a doubt the *pastel de bacalhau*, a fried salt cod cake with potatoes, eggs, and parsley, spooned into a quenelle shape and lowered into bubbling oil. We're almost as keen on *rissóis*, which are half moon–shaped pastries that are breaded and deep-fried. My favorite are *rissóis de camarão* (Shrimp Turnovers; page 74), in which the shrimp are bound in a lovely, creamy béchamel that oozes out when you bite it. Yes, I have burnt my tongue a fair few times over the years, so I urge you to be cautious— something I almost always forget when these are in front of me. Ouch.

There are also puff pastries with a center of cheese and ham, or spinach, as well as *chamuças* (samosas) and *croquetes* (croquettes). Some of these are breaded, while others are spooned straight into the fryer. Although most *salgados* are fried, we include *empadas* (small pies) among their number; these are often filled with chicken, duck, or pork.

The *sal* in *salgado* means "salt," and the Portuguese do have a fondness for salt that other nationalities sometimes find a bit too much. Salt is part of our heritage; centuries ago, the Vikings gave us a taste for our own salt and we've been curing cod and cooking with it ever since, so you might excuse us a little. When you're in Lisbon you can say *quero pouco sal*, I only want a little salt, or *sem sal*, without salt. For the recipes in this chapter I've gone easy on the salt.

The *salgados* here are a selection of my favorites and are ideal for a drinks party—you can fry them earlier in the afternoon, then heat them up in batches in the oven at 390°F/200°C (convection 355°F/180°C); this will be less smelly than frying everything in front of your guests. Sometimes, though, it's nice to do this just for yourself and your family or friends. One of my favorite things in the world is to fill, breadcrumb, and fry a batch of *rissóis de camarão* before eating them right there and then, when no one else is around, accompanied by a cold bottle of Super Bock or Sagres beer. It's nothing less than bliss.

Salt cod cakes 55
Pastéis de bacalhau

·

Runner bean fritters with clam broth 57
Peixinhos da horta

·

Chouriço and potato balls 58
Bolinhas de chouriço com batata

·

Duck pies 60
Empadas de pato vinha d'alhos

·

Pork and beef croquettes 64
Croquetes de carne

·

Fried pork crescents 67
Pastéis de massa tenra

·

Fried cornmeal with parsley 68
Milho frito

·

Green eggs 71
Ovos verdes

·

Shrimp turnovers 74
Rissóis de camarão

·

Spiced crab samosas 77
Chamuças de caranguejo

·

Salt cod fritters 78
Bolinhas bacalhau à Brás

Salt cod cakes
Pastéis de bacalhau

Makes about 18

1⅔ cups/400 ml extra-virgin olive oil

1 bay leaf

2 garlic cloves, crushed

½ long red chile, cut into chunks

2 (5-ounce/150 g) cured cod fillets
(page 97)

10 ounces/300 g floury potatoes,
such as russet

1 onion, finely chopped

Flaky sea salt and ground white pepper

2 eggs

A small handful of parsley leaves,
finely chopped

Vegetable oil, for frying

Lemon wedges, to serve

Salt cod cakes are one of the most popular Portuguese snacks, and they have been exported, along with our people, to many corners of the world. This is a simple, easy recipe that I really enjoy making. Instead of using salt cod, I cure my own fish, which makes it sweeter and less dry, so my little cakes are perhaps juicier than the ones you'll find in Lisbon. If you prefer to use salt cod, soak it in cold water for at least 2 to 3 days and pick it apart carefully.

Put the olive oil, bay leaf, 1 of the garlic cloves, and the chile in a pan over low heat and heat to 185°F/85°C, or until the oil just starts to bubble. Take care that it does not boil. Remove from the heat, wait a few minutes, then slide in the fish. After 15 minutes, the cod should be cooked and flaking nicely. Carefully transfer the fish to a plate, then gently flake it into bite-size chunks.

Cook the potatoes with their skins on in boiling salted water until they start falling apart. Drain and leave them to cool, then scoop out the flesh and mash it with a potato ricer or masher.

Heat the olive oil in a pan over medium heat, add the onion and remaining 1 clove garlic, and cook until soft. Season with salt and pepper, increase the heat, and cook for 5 minutes more, or until the onions caramelize.

In a bowl, combine the flaked cod, mashed potato, caramelized onion and garlic, eggs, and parsley to make a thick paste and season with salt and pepper. If you'd prefer not to taste raw eggs, just add it after seasoning. Shape the mixture: the traditional shape is a quenelle, which is made using two tablespoons, but you can also scoop out tablespoons or make little balls. Chill for 30 minutes on a baking sheet lined with baking parchment.

Fill a large heavy-bottomed pan one-third full with vegetable oil and heat it to 355°F/180°C, or until a cube of bread sizzles and turns golden brown almost immediately. Fry the cakes in small batches for 2 to 3 minutes, or until golden brown. Remove and drain on paper towels. I love to eat them right away with a squeeze of lemon.

Runner bean fritters with clam broth *Peixinhos da horta*

Serves 2 to 4

For the clam broth

3 tablespoons extra-virgin olive oil

2 garlic cloves, smashed

A bunch of cilantro, leaves and stalks separated and finely chopped

17 ounces/500 g live clams, purged and scrubbed

Freshly squeezed juice of 1 lemon

For the runner bean fritters

8 ounces/250 g runner beans or green beans, washed and thinly sliced diagonally

Clam meat, saved from the broth (optional)

1 small sweet onion, very thinly sliced

A handful of parsley, leaves finely chopped

⅔ cup/100 g rice flour

⅔ cup/150 ml dry white wine

Flaky sea salt

Vegetable oil, for frying

The name *peixinhos da horta* literally means "small fish from the vegetable garden," and I suspect it refers to the cooking method for this dish: we fry the beans tempura style, just as we often serve fish, until the coating is crisp but the beans inside are still tender. Here, the *peixinhos* are partnered with a lovely clam broth with olive oil, garlic, lemon, and cilantro, but they would also be delicious with a garlicky lemon and cilantro aioli (try the lemon aioli recipe on page 290, and stir in some chopped cilantro).

To make the broth — Heat the olive oil in a large shallow pan over low heat. Add the garlic and cilantro stalks and cook until fragrant. Add the clams and spread them out in a single layer, then cover and cook for 3 minutes, giving the pan a couple of shakes. After 3 minutes, discard any clams that do not open. Remove from the heat and stir in the lemon juice and cilantro leaves, reserving a handful for later. Remove the clams and reserve the broth. Remove the clam meat from the shells, then set it aside to use in the fritter mix, if you like.

To make the fritters — Mix together the runner beans, clam meat, onion, and parsley. In a separate bowl, whisk the rice flour with the white wine and season with salt. The batter should be quite runny so that it does not coat the beans too heavily. Don't let the batter sit for too long before using it, or the flour will settle at the bottom. Do not combine the batter and beans until you're ready to fry.

Fill a large heavy-bottomed pan one-third full with vegetable oil and heat it to 355°F/180°C, or until a cube of bread sizzles and turns golden brown almost immediately. Mix the the beans into the batter and carefully drop spoonfuls into the oil in small batches, then cook for 2 to 3 minutes, or until just golden brown at the edges. Remove with a slotted spoon and drain on paper towels. Serve immediately in a bowl with the clam broth and a little cilantro.

Chouriço and potato balls
Bolinhas de chouriço com batata

Makes about 15

3 floury potatoes (around 10 ounces/300 g),
    such as russet
2 tablespoons olive oil
2 onions, finely chopped
Flaky sea salt and ground white pepper
3½ ounces/100 g chouriço
    (skin removed), diced
1¾ ounces/50 g fine dried breadcrumbs
1 egg, beaten
Vegetable oil, for frying

Bolinhas **(the word literally means "marbles" and is used for several round-shaped pastries and snacks) are not a typical** *salgado* **but they are super tasty, so I had to include them here. This recipe works very well with the Portuguese cured sausage** *chouriço,* **but it will really sing if you use** *alheira,* **a fantastic smoked chicken sausage (page 191).**

Cook the potatoes in a large pan of boiling salted water until tender. Remove from the pan and set aside until cooled. Peel off the skins and mash the flesh with a fork.

Heat the olive oil in a pan, add the onions, and cook over medium heat for 10 minutes, or until softened. Season with salt and pepper. Add the *chouriço* and continue cooking until the onions caramelize. Remove the pan from the heat.

In a bowl, mix together the mashed potatoes and sautéed *chouriço* and onions. Stir in the breadcrumbs and egg. Shape the mixture into walnut-size balls and chill for 30 minutes.

Fill a large, heavy-bottomed pan one-third full with vegetable oil and heat it to 355°F/180°C, or until a cube of bread sizzles and turns golden brown almost immediately. Fry the balls in small batches for 2 to 3 minutes, or until golden brown. Remove with a slotted spoon and drain on paper towels. Serve warm.

Duck pies
Empadas de pato vinha d'alhos

Makes 15 to 20

For the dough
2 cups plus 2 tablespoons/
    300 g all-purpose flour
1 teaspoon fine sea salt
7 tablespoons/100 g butter
1 tablespoon olive oil
1 tablespoon duck fat

For the duck
2 duck legs
1 small onion, coarsely chopped
1 garlic clove, smashed
1 carrot, coarsely chopped
1 bay leaf
Flaky sea salt and ground white pepper

For the filling
1 tablespoon olive oil
1 tablespoon duck fat
1 cinnamon stick
1 star anise
3 strips orange zest
1 bay leaf
1 small onion, finely chopped
½ small fennel bulb, trimmed
    and finely chopped
1 garlic clove, crushed
3 tablespoons/50 ml Madeira
5 tablespoons/75 ml dry white wine
2 tablespoons/25 g butter
¼ cup/35 g all-purpose flour
Finely grated zest of 1 orange
A small bunch of parsley leaves,
    finely chopped
1 egg, beaten with a splash of milk

Empadas—little pies with various fillings—are a staple food in Lisbon. Over the years I've searched far and wide for the perfect empada, and now I've found it, filled with duck. The acidity of the wine and garlic sauce cuts deliciously through the richness of the duck and the pastry.

To make the dough — Sift the flour and salt into a bowl and rub in the butter. Stir in the olive oil and duck fat. Pour in about 6 tablespoons/90 to 100 ml of water and stir quickly to incorporate it to make a firm but pliable dough. Knead on a lightly floured surface for a few minutes. Wrap and chill for 1 hour.

To cook the duck — Put the duck legs in a pan with the onion, garlic, carrot, and bay leaf and season with salt and pepper. Simmer gently over low heat for 1 hour, or until tender, then remove and allow to cool slightly. Remove the meat from the bones and roughly chop the skin and meat. Reserve the liquid.

To make the filling — Heat the olive oil and duck fat in a pan over medium heat and add the cinnamon, star anise, orange zest strips, and bay leaf. Add the onion, fennel, and garlic and cook gently for 10 minutes, or until soft. Stir in the duck meat and skin, Madeira, and white wine and cook for a few minutes more. Taste for seasoning and leave to cool, then remove the spices, orange zest, and bay leaf.

Melt the butter in a pan over low heat, add the flour, and cook for a few minutes, or until light golden brown. Gradually stir in 1¼ cups/300 ml of the reserved cooking liquid, then bring to a boil and simmer until you have a thick sauce. Stir it into the filling along with the grated orange zest and parsley.

Preheat the oven to 390°F/200°C (convection 355°F/180°C). Divide the dough in half and roll each half out to around ⅛ inch/3 mm thick. Use a large cookie cutter to cut one half into circles big enough to cover the holes of a muffin tin or small individual pie tins with an excess of about ¼ inch/5 mm. Cut the other half into smaller circles to fit on top as lids. Line the tins with the larger circles and put a heaping tablespoon of filling inside each one. Brush the edges with the beaten egg and put the smaller circle on top. Pinch the edges together to seal and crimp them, using a fork if necessary, and brush the tops with egg. Poke a steam hole in the tops. Bake for 15 minutes, then remove the pies from the tins, transfer them to a wire rack, and bake for 10 minutes more. They are best eaten 15 to 20 minutes after they come out of the oven, when they're still warm but the duck has rested a little.

Pork and beef croquettes
Croquetes de carne

Makes about 20

For the filling
2 tablespoons olive oil
1 onion, finely diced
2 garlic cloves, crushed
1 carrot, finely diced
1 bay leaf
Flaky sea salt and ground white pepper
5½ ounces/160 g good-quality ground pork
5½ ounces/160 g good-quality ground beef
5 slices (1 ounce/30 g) Ibérico ham, finely
    chopped
A splash of Madeira
A splash of brandy
A pinch of freshly grated nutmeg
2½ tablespoons/35 g butter
¼ cup/35 g all-purpose flour
2 cups/500 ml whole milk

For the coating
¾ cup/100 g all-purpose flour
4 eggs, beaten
7 ounces/200 g breadcrumbs

Vegetable oil, for frying
Portuguese-style mustard (see page 20),
to serve

The best *croquetes* have a wonderfully deep, rich flavor and a beautiful contrast between the unctuous middle and the crisp coating. My favorites are made with a secret family recipe at a *pastelaria* in Estoril, so I've had to rely on my intuition to develop this recipe. Thankfully, it's so good that I no longer have to trek to Portugal every time the craving strikes.

To make the filling — Heat the olive oil in a large frying pan over medium heat, add the onion, garlic, carrot, and bay leaf, and cook gently for 10 minutes, or until soft. Season with salt and pepper, add the pork, beef, and Ibérico ham, increase the heat, and cook until browned. Drain off any excess fat, keeping a little in for flavor. Taste for seasoning and add the Madeira, brandy, and nutmeg to your taste. Remove the bay leaf and set aside.

Melt the butter in a pan over medium heat, stir in the flour, and cook for a few minutes until light golden brown. Pour in the milk gradually, whisking constantly, then bring to a boil and cook for 2 minutes. Reduce the heat and gently simmer for 10 minutes, or until thickened. Stir this into the meat filling and taste for seasoning. Transfer to a plate and leave to cool, covered with plastic wrap to prevent a skin from forming.

To coat the croquettes — Put the flour, eggs, and breadcrumbs into three separate shallow bowls. Shape tablespoons of the filling lightly with your hands into rough cylinders. Dip each one in the flour, then in the egg, and shake gently to get rid of any excess. Dip in the breadcrumbs and repeat the process (I prefer to use a double coating for a better shape). Reshape after coating, then chill for 30 minutes.

Fill a large heavy-bottomed pan one-third full with vegetable oil and heat it to 355°F/180°C, or until a cube of bread sizzles and turns golden brown almost immediately. Fry the croquettes in batches, turning as needed, for 3 to 4 minutes, or until golden brown. Don't overcrowd the pan or they won't cook evenly. Remove and drain on paper towels, then serve by themselves or with Portuguese-style mustard.

Fried pork crescents
Pastéis de massa tenra

Makes 15 to 20

For the dough

2⅓ cups/330 g all-purpose flour,
    plus extra for dusting

1 teaspoon fine sea salt

½ ounce/15 g soft pork fat or lard, melted

⅓ cup/80 ml dry white wine

4 teaspoons/20 ml olive oil

For the filling

1 tablespoon olive oil

2 tablespoons/25 g rendered pork fat
    or lard, plus 1 teaspoon

2 ounces/50 g chouriço (skin removed),
    diced

½ small onion, finely diced

1 small garlic clove, crushed

Flaky sea salt and ground white pepper

A pinch of freshly grated nutmeg

5 ounces/150 g good-quality ground pork

1¼ cups/300 ml pork stock

A splash of brandy

A splash of sherry vinegar

A small handful of parsley leaves,
    finely chopped

3 tablespoons/30 g all-purpose flour

Vegetable oil, for frying

Pastéis de massa tenra **recipes are often passed down the generations by grandmothers, but because mine are sadly no longer here, my friend Lica Pedroso has shared her exquisite version with me; it has a thin, puffy crust that encloses a succulent pork filling. The** *chouriço* **adds a rich and smoky kick.**

To make the dough — Sift the flour and salt into a bowl and stir in the pork fat. Make a well in the center and pour in ¼ cup/70 ml of water, the white wine, and the olive oil. Bring it together to form a smooth dough, then knead it on a lightly floured surface for 10 minutes (you need a bit of elbow grease here). Cover and leave to rest for 30 minutes.

To make the filling — Heat the olive oil and 1 teaspoon of pork fat in a pan over medium heat. Add the *chouriço* and cook for a few minutes until the fat melts. Add the onion and garlic and cook until soft, then season with salt, pepper, and nutmeg. Stir in the ground pork and cook until golden brown. Drain off the excess fat, keeping some in for flavor, then add a good ¾ cup/200 ml of the pork stock and simmer gently for 20 minutes. Taste for seasoning and add the brandy, sherry vinegar, and parsley.

Melt the remaining 2 tablespoons/25 g pork fat in a pan over low heat, stir in the flour, and cook for 2 to 3 minutes, or until light golden brown. Gradually stir in the remaining ½ cup/100 ml pork stock and bring to a boil, stirring constantly. Reduce the heat and simmer gently for 5 minutes, or until thickened. Fold the sauce into the filling and leave to cool.

On a lightly floured work surface, roll out the dough to around ¹⁄₁₀ inch/2 mm thick. Use a 4-inch/10-cm fluted cookie cutter to cut out circles. Place a heaping teaspoon of filling in the middle of each circle, leaving a border around the edge. Fold the circles in half and seal the edges well. Chill for 30 minutes.

Fill a large heavy-bottomed pan one-third full with vegetable oil and heat it to 355°F/180°C, or until a cube of bread sizzles and turns golden brown almost immediately. Fry the crescents in small batches for 2 to 3 minutes, or until golden brown. Remove and drain on paper towels. Serve hot or at room temperature.

Fried cornmeal with parsley
Milho frito

Serves 4

1 tablespoon rendered pork fat or lard
4 tablespoons olive oil
1 garlic clove, finely crushed
¾ cup/180 ml vegetable or chicken stock
2 tablespoons/30 g butter
1½ cups/180 g fine cornmeal or polenta
A large bunch of parsley,
    leaves finely chopped
Fine sea salt and ground white pepper
Lemon wedges, to serve
Piri piri oil (page 156), to serve

Milho frito, **a kind of crispy cornmeal cake that is a little bit like polenta, is originally from Madeira, but is enjoyed throughout Lisbon. It's simple to make and can be eaten as a snack on its own or as a side dish; it would be nice with the Beef Skewers with Chouriço and Bay Leaves (page 220). It is incredibly versatile and stores well, so you can make a large batch of the batter and cut it into squares once it's set, then chill or freeze them until you're ready to fry.**

Heat the pork fat and 1 tablespoon of the olive oil in a pan over low heat. Add the garlic and cook until fragrant. Pour in the stock, add the butter, and bring to a boil. Pour the cornmeal into another pan and, whisking constantly, pour the liquid over the cornmeal in a continuous stream. Bring to a boil and cook gently for 4 to 5 minutes, or until it thickens. Remove the pan from the heat, stir in most of the parsley, and season with salt and pepper. Pour into a lightly oiled baking sheet and leave it to set until firm. Cut into squares.

Heat the remaining 3 tablespoons olive oil in a large frying pan and fry the squares in batches for 2 to 3 minutes on each side, or until golden brown. Remove and drain on paper towels. Serve warm, scattered with the remaining parsley if you like, with lemon wedges and piri piri oil on the side.

Green eggs
Ovos verdes

Makes 12

7 eggs
1 small shallot, finely chopped
5 slices good-quality roast ham,
    finely chopped
A large handful of parsley leaves,
    finely chopped
1 tablespoon Portuguese-style mustard
    (see page 20), plus extra to serve
Flaky sea salt and ground white pepper
¾ cup/100 g all-purpose flour
3 eggs, beaten with a dash of milk
5 ounces/150 g fine dried breadcrumbs
Vegetable oil, for frying

Green eggs are quite close to Scotch eggs, really. The eggs are hard-boiled and cut in half, then the yolks are scooped out and mixed with lots of parsley—which creates the green color—plus mustard, shallots, and ham. This mixture is then shaped around the egg whites before they are battered and quick-fried until crisp. They are pretty amazing. I recommend serving them with a bit of mustard and lemon on the side.

Put the eggs in a pan and cover with cold water, bring to a boil, then cover and turn off the heat. Leave for 10 minutes, then remove and cool in iced water to stop the cooking. Once cooled, peel the eggs. (I find that they sometimes break a little when you peel them, so I always allow an extra one. Any leftover egg white can be finely chopped and added to the yolk mixture or used for another recipe.)

Cut the eggs in half lengthwise, remove the yolks, and put them in a bowl. Add the shallot, ham, parsley, and mustard and mash well. Taste for seasoning (you may not need to add salt if the ham is quite salty).

Take about 1 tablespoon of the mixture and mold it on top of an egg white, filling the yolk cavity and molding it on top so that it looks like a whole egg. There should be enough to cover about 12 halves. Chill them for 30 minutes.

Put the flour, beaten egg, and breadcrumbs into separate bowls. Roll each cooked egg in flour, then beaten egg (shaking off any excess), then breadcrumbs. Roll them in the egg and breadcrumbs again. This double coating helps prevent the egg white and yolk mixture from separating during frying. Chill them for 30 minutes.

Fill a large heavy-bottomed pan one-third full with vegetable oil and heat it to 355°F/180°C, or until a cube of bread sizzles and turns golden brown almost immediately. Fry the eggs in batches for 2 to 3 minutes, or until golden brown. Don't overcrowd the pan or they won't cook evenly. Remove and drain on paper towels. Serve right away with a little Portuguese-style mustard to dip.

Café Culture

Cafés are part of the very fabric of Lisbon—not just physically, but emotionally, too. From elaborate Art Nouveau establishments to the most basic little *pastelarias* (pastry shops) with a few metal chairs and Formica tables, they play a crucial part in everyday life here. They are a place for people to meet, chat, exchange ideas, or sit quietly in contemplation of the world, through the window or with a newspaper.

Whether they arrive with the intention of lingering or simply of spending a few minutes at the counter with a *bica*, most *lisboetas* visit a café or *pastelaria* almost every day. A *bica* is much like an espresso, slightly larger in volume though still served in a very small cup, and usually drunk black. You can also ask for *um café cheio*, basically a *bica* topped up with hot water; *uma carioca*, which is like an Americano; *uma galão*, a long coffee with a lot of milk, usually served in a glass; or *um garoto*, which is the same size as a *bica* but is half coffee and half hot milk. A *pingado* or *bica pingada* is a *bica* with just a touch of milk. If it's your first

time in Lisbon, you'll want to seek out A Brasileira, an iconic café that opened its glass-paned doors in 1905 and was once a magnet for the country's best writers, including our most famous poet, Fernando Pessoa. His statue sits, cross-legged, outside on the terrace, which is a nice spot to rest and absorb the comings and goings of the Chiado neighborhood, but you really must step inside to appreciate the full glory. Carved redwood panels line the walls, intersecting with vast mirrors, and lovely brass hand and foot rails run along the counter. Of course, it's a tourist trap—it couldn't be anything else, with its history and its prime location in the heart of historic Lisbon—but it's a gem all the same.

Another classic of the era is Café Versailles, a little way out of the center in the Saldanha neighborhood. It's modeled on the French palace of the same name and, as you might imagine, is incredibly ornate. Again, mirrors and moldings are everywhere and the waiters are old-school, all liveried up and rather touchingly formal. My friend Célia Pedroso, a journalist who now leads food tours all over the city, swears that this place has the best *pastéis de nata* (custard tarts) anywhere and, given that she's a total pastry addict, I'm inclined to believe her.

Of course, anyone coming to Lisbon for the first time is bound to make a pilgrimage to Pastéis de Belém, the café that gave birth to the famous *pastéis*. They are said to make more than twenty thousand custard tarts a day, and the recipe is still a secret. The pastries were first produced in 1837 from a

recipe passed on from the next-door monastery, Mosteiro dos Jerónimos. Although I don't personally feel that these are the best *pastéis* in the city, I still recommend a visit to the warren of rooms decorated in blue-and-white tiles depicting seventeenth-century life, where you can watch through a glass window as the *pastéis* are made.

Café culture in Lisbon grew out of the ashes of a terrible earthquake in 1755, when the forward-thinking prime minister, the Marquis de Pombal, encouraged new cafés to open and supported the notion that they could become a place where intellectuals, writers, and artists could get together to engage in debate—or sometimes heated argument. This kind of social gathering was known as a *tertúlia*, almost like a literary salon, and they were—no surprises here—a male stronghold. But the Salazar dictatorship discouraged people from meeting in groups and so from 1932 to 1974 this open merging of minds and ideas over coffee was stifled.

This sad suffocation extended to the beautiful *quiosques* (kiosks) that you see all over Lisbon. Created in iron, the design of many *quiosques* reflects our Moorish history, and are adorned with beautiful filigree latticework awnings and decorative domes. The first was erected in the main square at Rossio in 1869, and they then began to appear all around the city. They sold food, drink, cigarettes, and newspapers, and were a perfect way to combine the *lisboeta* love of outdoor life with our passion for just being together. All this changed during

Salazar's Estado Novo (New State), and even when the dictatorship was over, these beautiful structures stayed shuttered up and in decline until about eight years ago. But then, quite brilliantly, some young and exciting entrepreneurs decided that the *quiosques* should be revived and now there are one hundred of them up and running again all across the city. Some of them have *miradouros* (golden views) looking out across Lisbon. One of the most popular is located in the middle of the Praça de Luís de Camões in Chiado; my own favorite is perhaps the one in Jardim Botto Machado, right in the middle of the Feira da Ladra (literally, "thieves' market"), a flea market that folds itself out onto the streets all around this area on Tuesdays and Saturdays. It was here that I ate the almond and orange tart that inspired the recipe on page 31.

On a hot Lisbon day or night, one of the best things you can do is find a *quiosque* under the fragrant purple blossoms of a jacaranda tree and sit with an iced *porto tónico*, the typically Portuguese drink of white port served with tonic and ice. Back in 1867, the building application for that very first *quiosque* asserted that the structure's duty was simply to "beautify the street." To my mind, the *quiosques* of Lisbon beautify not only the street, but also the daily lives of *lisboetas*.

Shrimp turnovers
Rissóis de camarão

Makes about 36

3 cups/750 ml whole milk, plus extra

2 bay leaves

20 to 25 raw jumbo shrimp, shells
    and heads on

1 tablespoon olive oil

For the pastry

2 tablespoons/30 g butter

2 cups/280 g all-purpose flour, plus extra

1 teaspoon salt

1 teaspoon ground white pepper

¼ teaspoon cayenne pepper

½ teaspoon smoked paprika

For the filling

1 tablespoon olive oil

2 tablespoons/30 g butter

½ small onion, very finely chopped

Flaky sea salt and ground white pepper

1 garlic clove, crushed

1 ripe plum tomato, peeled, seeded,
    and finely chopped

A pinch of freshly grated nutmeg

½ teaspoon smoked paprika

¼ cup/30 g cornstarch

A squeeze of lemon juice, plus lemon
    wedges to serve

A small bunch of cilantro, leaves
    finely chopped

A small bunch of parsley, leaves
    finely chopped

1 egg yolk, beaten

For the coating

2 eggs, beaten

3½ ounces/100 g dried breadcrumbs

Vegetable oil, for frying

I utterly adore *rissóis*. I once cooked up a batch that were so special—warm and crispy on the outside and oozing with juicy shrimp filling inside—that I began daydreaming of a restaurant in London that might do those little treasures justice. Happily, that reverie became a reality in the form of Taberna do Mercado, and here is the recipe that inspired it. Serve the *rissóis* with plenty of freshly squeezed lemon.

Bring the milk and bay leaves to a simmer in a large pan. Poach the shrimp in the milk for 2 minutes, or until cooked through. Remove the shrimp, reserving the milk, peel them, and twist off the heads. Set aside the shells and heads. To devein the shrimp, use a small knife to make a slit along the middle of the back, then pull out the veins. Roughly chop the bodies and set aside.

Heat the olive oil in a large pan over medium heat. Add the shrimp shells and heads and cook until lightly toasted. Pour in the reserved milk and bring to a simmer. Remove from the heat, cover, and leave to infuse for 30 minutes. Strain through a sieve, pressing the heads and shells with the back of a spoon to extract maximum flavor. Set aside 2 cups/500 ml infused milk for the pastry and 1 cup/250 ml for the filling, topping up with a little extra milk if needed.

To make the pastry — Heat the butter and the 2 cups/500 ml of infused milk in a pan. Sift the flour and seasonings onto a large sheet of baking parchment. Just before the milk starts to boil, quickly tip the flour into the pan, using the parchment as a funnel. Beat vigorously until the dough starts to pull away from the sides of the pan and forms a ball. Take the pan off the heat and turn the dough out onto a lightly floured surface. Let it cool for a few minutes, then lightly knead until smooth and springing back when gently pressed. Cover with a clean kitchen towel.

To make the filling — Heat the olive oil and butter in a large pan over medium heat, add the onion, and cook for about 10 minutes, or until soft. Season with salt and pepper, add the garlic, and cook until fragrant. Stir in the tomato and the 1 cup/250 ml of infused milk and bring to a boil. Reduce the heat to low and stir in the nutmeg and paprika. Taste for seasoning. →

→ In a small bowl, mix the cornstarch with a splash of water to make a smooth paste. Stir this into the pan and simmer gently, stirring constantly, until the sauce thickens enough to coat the back of the spoon. Add the chopped shrimp and a dash of lemon juice along with the cilantro and parsley, then taste for seasoning. Spread the filling out on a baking sheet, cover with plastic wrap, and leave to cool to room temperature.

Divide the dough in half. Roll out each half on a lightly floured surface to around ⅛ inch/3 mm thick. Cut out 3½-inch/8-cm circles from the dough with a fluted pastry cutter (you should get about 36). Cover them with a kitchen towel to keep them from drying out. Put a heaping teaspoon of the filling in the center of each circle and lightly brush egg yolk around the edge. Fold in half to enclose the filling, like making a small pasty. Squeeze the edges together to seal and gently push out any air pockets. Put them on a baking sheet and chill them while making the rest.

To coat the turnovers — Put the whole eggs in one bowl and the breadcrumbs in another. Dip each turnover into the egg, shake off the excess, and dip in the breadcrumbs.

Fill a large, heavy-bottomed pan one-third full with vegetable oil and heat it to 355°F/180°C, or until a cube of bread sizzles and turns golden brown almost immediately. Fry the turnovers in small batches for about 4 minutes, or until the pastry is cooked through. Remove and drain on paper towels. Serve immediately with lemon wedges and an ice-cold beer.

Spiced crab samosas
Chamuças de caranguejo

Makes about 24

2 tablespoons grapeseed oil

1 small red pepper, seeded
and finely chopped

1 small onion, finely diced

⅓ ounce/10 g fresh ginger,
finely chopped

1 garlic clove, crushed

½ teaspoon smoked paprika

½ teaspoon ground cumin

½ teaspoon ground white pepper

½ teaspoon ground turmeric

A pinch of cayenne pepper

2 tablespoons tamarind paste

1 small plum tomato, finely chopped

7 ounces/200 g white crabmeat

A small handful of cilantro,
leaves finely chopped

Flaky sea salt

Freshly squeezed lemon juice

12 spring roll wrappers

Vegetable oil, for frying

Chamuças (samosas) have been beloved in Portugal ever since our explorers traveled to India in the sixteenth century and brought back this spiced-up version of a traditional Portuguese snack. I'm particularly fond of *chamuças* made with seafood—which aren't as common as the meat-filled variety—and my friend Jesus Lee serves the best ones at his small Goan restaurant Jesus é Goes. Pay him a visit and tell him that I sent you; you'll be extremely well looked after.

Heat the grapeseed oil in a pan over medium heat, add the red pepper, and cook until soft and gently caramelized. Add the onion, ginger, and garlic and cook for 10 minutes, or until soft. Stir in all the spices and the tamarind paste and cook until the mixture starts to sizzle; the aim is to toast the spices for maximum flavor. Add the tomato and cook for another few minutes, then stir in the crabmeat and cilantro. Taste for seasoning and adjust with salt and lemon juice, then cook for another few minutes. Transfer the filling to a plate and leave to cool.

Cut each spring roll wrapper into two rectangular strips about 3½ by 7 inches/9 by 18 cm. Place a heaping teaspoon of the filling at one end of each strip, leaving a ¾-inch/2-cm border. Take the bottom right-hand corner and fold it diagonally to the left to enclose the filling and form a triangle. Fold it up again along the upper edge of the triangle, then repeat the folding until you reach the end of the strip. Moisten the edges with water to help seal it. Chill for 30 minutes.

Fill a large heavy-bottomed pan one-third full with vegetable oil and heat it to 355°F/180°C, or until a cube of bread sizzles and turns golden brown almost immediately. Fry the *chamuças* in small batches for 2 to 3 minutes, or until pale golden. Remove with a slotted spoon and drain on paper towels.

Salt cod fritters
Bolinhas bacalhau à Brás

Makes about 10

¼ cup/40 g cornstarch

3 tablespoons/40 ml dry white wine

5 ounces/150 g leftover cooked bacalhau
à Brás (page 200)

A small handful of parsley, finely chopped

For the dipping sauce

A large handful of parsley leaves,
finely chopped

A large handful of cilantro leaves,
finely chopped

½ small long red chile, finely chopped

½ teaspoon smoked paprika

1 teaspoon honey

4 tablespoons extra-virgin olive oil

1 tablespoon sliced almonds, lightly toasted

Freshly squeezed lemon juice

Flaky sea salt and ground white pepper

Vegetable oil, for frying

I discovered the flavors of Goa when my father took me to a Goan restaurant in Lisbon as a very small boy. One of my favorite things on the menu was *bhajis*—I loved the crunch and creaminess. One day, after making *bacalhau à Brás*, I looked at the leftovers and thought of those *bhajis*. I fried the cod mix up and the result was stunning—it's worth making extra mix especially for this recipe. For the dip I replaced the traditional coconut flavoring with almonds, which grow in abundance in Portugal.

In a small bowl, mix the cornstarch and white wine into a paste. Stir it into the leftover *bacalhau à Brás* along with the parsley.

To make the dipping sauce — Combine all the sauce ingredients except the almonds. Stir in the almonds at the end, then taste and season as required with lemon juice, salt, and white pepper to make a sharp, herby sauce.

Fill a large, heavy-bottomed pan one-third full with vegetable oil and heat it to 355°F/180°C, or until a cube of bread sizzles and turns golden brown almost immediately. Gently drop tablespoons of the batter into the oil and fry for 2 minutes, or until golden brown. Cook them in batches so as not to overcrowd the pan. Remove with a slotted spoon and drain on paper towels, then serve immediately with the dipping sauce on the side.

Alm

OÇO

Modern Lisbon, like most other capital cities across the world, is a time-pressed place at lunchtime. Nevertheless, that horrible culture of picking up sandwiches from a fridge and running back to the office simply doesn't exist here. In fact, most *lisboetas* would laugh you down if you even dared to suggest eating something so unnaturally cold and clearly made at least twelve hours ago in a factory miles away. Yes, they might grab a *bifana* or a *prego* (a hot pork or beef sandwich) at the counter, but it will be cooked fresh before their eyes, served hot, and probably accompanied by a small bowl of soup.

In Portugal we're often really hungry by lunchtime—we don't tend to eat much for breakfast—so this meal is still a reasonably big affair in terms of what people eat, however pushed for time. That's why *tascas* do a good, brisk trade between midday and two o'clock. Many people like to order three courses: soup, a dish of fish or meat served with rice and potatoes, and a dessert and a coffee. Those in a hurry will wolf down a hot *prato do dia* (dish of the day) and leave feeling satisfied.

Soup is an important element of lunch, and for many people in Lisbon this is a main source of vegetables—it's a shame, but our country's cooks have never bothered much with vegetables, as many vegetarian travelers discover to their horror. For a long time Portugal was a deeply impoverished country, and its people found ways to eke out the small amounts of food they had by creating fabulous soups. The very idea of eating soup from a can is ridiculous to the Portuguese—not least because it's lazy and extravagant. *Caldo verde* (page 89), which rose to become our most popular soup, is traditionally made with *chouriço* or *linguiça* sausage, shredded cabbage, potatoes, and water. It's incredibly simple, using only a few cheap ingredients, but it could easily be described as Portugal in a bowl. My recipe for Old-Style Onion Soup (page 86) was inspired by a deliciously sweet and creamy version that I tasted in a restaurant more than thirty years ago, and which has lingered in my mind ever since.

In the past, Portugal would come to a standstill for a couple of hours every day at lunchtime: the shutters were pulled down and people scuttled off to the local *tasca* or back home to eat at the table with their families. For the older generation, lunch remains the most important meal of the day. Of course, we all like to spend a few hours relishing it when we can, so I have included some recipes here for dishes that take a little longer to cook but are the kind you'll want to enjoy slowly once you have them on the table—I'm thinking of the rather complicated but glorious Fish Soup (page 104), or my Octopus with Smashed Potatoes, Olive Oil, and Piso (page 98). There's a Portuguese saying that lunch takes two hours: one hour for eating and one hour for talking. That's my favorite kind of lunch.

Baked salt cod with caramelized onions and potatoes 111
Bacalhau à Gomes de Sá

·

Shrimp bread porridge 113
Açorda de gambas

·

Monkfish and chouriço cataplana 116
Cataplana de tamboril

·

Sausage and cabbage rolls with tomato sauce 118
Salsichas com couve lombarda

·

Roasted orange-rubbed pork belly with fennel 120
Barriga de porco assada com laranja

·

Roast kid goat 125
Cabrito assado no forno

·

Café-style steak 126
Bife à café

·

Chicken and rice congee 132
Canja de galinha do campo

·

Grilled piri piri chicken with potato chips 135
Frango na brasa com piri piri

·

Slow-simmered bean, cabbage, and pork stew 138
Feijoada

Old-style onion soup

Sopa de cebola à antiga portuguesa

Serves 4

3 tablespoons olive oil,
    plus extra for drizzling
4 tablespoons/50 g butter
4 white and 4 yellow onions, thinly sliced
4 shallots, thinly sliced
4 teaspoons/20 ml brandy, plus extra
    to serve
3 tablespoons/50 ml Madeira, plus extra
    to serve
3½ cups/800 ml chicken or vegetable stock
4 slices sourdough or other rustic loaf
¼ cup/60 ml light cream
Flaky sea salt, ground white pepper,
    and cracked black pepper
A splash of sherry vinegar
1¾ ounces/50 g queijo da Ilha (or similar
    hard cheese such as Parmesan), grated
Extra-virgin olive oil, to serve

This is a comforting dish that requires little preparation. It makes the most of different types of onions and shallots, and the addition of brandy and Madeira creates a deep, rich flavor. If you can get your hands on some Portuguese *queijo da Ilha* (or *queijo São Jorge*), this is a great way to use it.

Heat the olive oil and butter in a large pan over medium heat, add the onions and shallots, cover, and cook for 10 minutes, or until soft and juicy. Pour the brandy, Madeira, and stock into the pan and stir well. Bring to a boil, then reduce the heat. Cover with a lid and simmer gently for 45 minutes, stirring occasionally, adding a little extra stock or water if needed.

Preheat the oven to 430°F/220°C (convection 390°F/200°C). Drizzle the bread with olive oil on each side. Bake on a baking sheet for 5 minutes, or until golden brown.

Remove about 4 tablespoons of the onions and shallots from the pan and set aside. Add the cream to the pan and blend the soup with an immersion blender. Season with salt and white pepper, then stir in a little extra brandy, Madeira, and a splash of sherry vinegar. Transfer to a tureen and keep warm.

Serve the soup in warmed shallow bowls. Put a slice of toast in each bowl and sprinkle it with cheese, then top with the reserved onions and shallots. Pour the soup over the toast along with some more cheese, a glug of extra-virgin olive oil, and cracked black pepper.

Kale soup with chouriço and potatoes *Caldo verde*

Serves 4

3 tablespoons olive oil

5 ounces/150 g chouriço (skin removed), diced, plus a few thin slices to garnish

2 onions, finely chopped

2 garlic cloves, crushed

1 bay leaf

Flaky sea salt and ground white pepper

4 potatoes, such as Yukon gold or similar, peeled and diced into small pieces

6 cups/1.5 L chicken stock or water

7 ounces/200 g kale, finely chopped

Extra-virgin olive oil, to serve

4 slices Cornbread (page 299), sourdough, or other rustic loaf, toasted, buttered, and cut into small pieces (optional)

Good-quality white wine vinegar, to serve

Caldo verde **is one of Portugal's most special, heartwarming dishes. The quality of the** *chouriço* **and the potatoes makes a big difference, so get the best you can. In Portugal, a type of cabbage called** *couve galega* **is used, but here I have gone for kale, which enhances the beautiful jade color. Traditionally,** *caldo verde* **is made with water, but I prefer to use chicken stock for a denser flavor—my compatriots will kill me, but I am prepared to stand my ground.**

Heat the olive oil in a pan over medium heat. Add the *chouriço* and cook for a couple of minutes, then add the onions, garlic, and bay leaf, season with salt and pepper, and cook until the onions are soft. Stir in the potatoes and sweat for a few minutes, stirring so the potatoes don't stick. Pour in the stock and simmer gently over low heat until the potatoes are soft. Remove a few tablespoons of the potatoes and set aside.

Add half the kale to the soup and simmer for a few minutes. Remove the bay leaf, take the soup off the heat, and blend until smooth with an immersion blender. (Traditionally the soup is not blended, but I like to blend it and add some more fresh kale at the end.) Return the pan to the heat and taste for seasoning. Add the reserved potatoes and remaining kale and simmer for a few minutes.

Ladle the soup into bowls. Finish with some thinly sliced *chouriço*, extra-virgin olive oil, and pieces of toast. As it can be quite a heavy soup, I like to add a splash of white wine vinegar to cut through the richness.

Tomato soup
Sopa de tomate

Serves 4

5 tablespoons extra-virgin olive oil,
  plus extra for drizzling

1 red onion, sliced into ⅛-inch/
  3 to 4 mm rings

2 yellow onions, sliced into ⅛-inch/
  3 to 4 mm rings

Flaky sea salt and ground white pepper

3 bay leaves

2 garlic cloves, crushed

1 tablespoon sherry vinegar,
  plus a little to serve

2 tablespoons Madeira, plus a little to serve

2¾ pounds/1.3 kg tomatoes (a mixture of
  types), coarsely chopped

4 slices sourdough or other rustic loaf,
  thickly sliced

A small handful of mint leaves

A few thin slices of lardo or a poached
  egg per person (optional)

When I was growing up I used to spend long, carefree summer days at my grandmother's beach house in Costa da Caparica, and when tomatoes were in peak season we would make soup. Nowadays I put a little toast in the bottom of the bowl and scatter some fresh mint leaves on top, and as the soup is ladled into the bowl the vibrant smell of tomatoes meeting mint takes me straight back to those days.

Try to find the best, ripest tomatoes you can for this. I like a selection of vine-ripened plum and heirloom tomatoes (yellow, green, zebra); always use what you love. It is a thick and chunky soup—if you'd prefer it more liquid, you can top it up with chicken or vegetable stock, tomato water, or even plain water.

You can also add rendered pork fat or chunks of *lardo* to the olive oil in the pan, but feel free to keep it vegetarian (I know which I prefer). Any leftovers could be turned into pasta sauce or served alongside a nice piece of grilled sea bass or mackerel.

Heat the olive oil in a large, wide pan over low heat, add the red and yellow onions, and cook for 10 minutes, or until soft and juicy. Season with salt and pepper. Add the bay leaf and garlic and cook for 2 minutes, or until fragrant. Add the sherry vinegar and Madeira, increase the heat to medium, and simmer for 2 more minutes to burn off some of the alcohol. Stir in the chopped tomatoes. Cook, covered, over medium heat for 10 minutes, or until the tomatoes have broken down a bit but are not mushy.

Preheat the oven to 430°F/220°C (convection 390°F/200°C). Drizzle each side of the bread with olive oil, place on a baking sheet, and bake for 5 minutes, or until golden brown.

Taste the soup for seasoning, adding a dash of sherry vinegar and Madeira if needed. To serve, place a slice of toast in each bowl with a few mint leaves on top and ladle the soup over. Finish with a few slices of *lardo* or a poached egg.

Cilantro-marinated fava beans
Favas de coentrada

Serves 4

1 egg

2 slices sourdough or other rustic loaf

2 tablespoons olive oil, plus extra
    for toasting the bread

7 ounces/200 g shelled fresh fava beans

1 shallot, finely chopped

1 garlic clove, crushed

A small handful of cilantro, leaves and
    stalks separated and finely chopped

Flaky sea salt and ground white pepper

Freshly squeezed juice and finely grated
    zest of 1 lemon

Chardonnay vinegar or good-quality white
    wine vinegar

Extra-virgin olive oil

Fava beans are most commonly used in their dried form in meat stews. That approach is tasty but very heavy, and fails to show off the beauty of the beans in their natural state. Instead, try this salad in spring, when fava beans first come into season and are young and bright and wonderful. It's lovely with grilled fish.

Put the egg in a pan of cold salted water and heat until it comes to a rolling boil. Remove from the heat and let the egg sit, covered, in the pan for 10 minutes. It should be hard-boiled with a slightly creamy but set yolk. Remove and put it in iced water to stop the cooking. Once cooled, peel and separate the white from the yolk. Finely grate the white and yolk, keeping them separate, and set aside.

Preheat the oven to 430°F/220°C (convection 390°F/200°C). Put the bread on a baking sheet and drizzle both sides with olive oil. Toast the bread until golden brown and crispy and, once cooled, coarsely chop it into coarse breadcrumbs.

Separate the big fava beans from the little ones. Peel the big ones (if necessary, plunge them into boiling water for 30 seconds, then drain and plunge them straight into iced water; this makes them a little easier to peel). Mix together the shallot, garlic, and cilantro stalks and season with salt and pepper.

Heat the 2 tablespoons olive oil in a frying pan over medium heat, add the shallot and cilantro paste, and cook until light golden brown. Add half the lemon juice. Turn the heat down to low and let it cook gently. Taste for seasoning; it may need more lemon juice. When the shallot and garlic are soft, add the fava beans and stir well. Take the pan off the heat and add a splash of vinegar. Add the cilantro leaves, lemon zest, and breadcrumbs, drizzle with a little extra-virgin olive oil, and sprinkle the grated egg white and yolk on top.

Hearty cod and cilantro broth
Açorda de bacalhau

Serves 2

For the cured cod

7 tablespoons/90 g superfine sugar

3½ tablespoons/60 g fine sea salt

Aromatics of your choice, such as bay
   leaves, coriander seeds, cilantro,
   parsley, orange and lemon zest, fennel
   seeds, black peppercorns, and perhaps
   a cinnamon stick for warmth

2 (5-ounce/150 g) skinless, pinboned cod
   fillets of an even thickness (the top,
   fatter part of the loin is ideal)

For the cod broth

2 tablespoons olive oil

7 ounces/200 g cod trimmings (ask your
   fishmonger)

2 garlic cloves, crushed

For the açorda

3 tablespoons olive oil

2 garlic cloves, crushed

A small bunch of cilantro, stalks
   finely chopped and leaves picked

Flaky sea salt and ground white pepper

2 slices sourdough or other rustic loaf

A handful of mint leaves

Extra-virgin olive oil, to serve

Açorda was invented during times of deep poverty, when ingredients had to be stretched in unfathomable ways. But despite its frugality, it's a soup we Portuguese truly love. A pan of fish stock mixed with garlic, cilantro, and olive oil, poured over a nice piece of cod and a slice of stale sourdough bread, is a brilliant example of how simple yet full of flavor our cooking can be.

I love to cure fish because it draws the moisture out of the flesh, which means it has a nicer texture and cooks more evenly. I use a ratio of 6 parts sugar to 4 parts salt (by weight), which enhances the natural sweetness of the fish. You can also add other flavorings, depending on the final dish (see left for suggestions). The possibilities are endless, so experiment! You could try curing halibut, bream, bass, mackerel, or sole and matching them with different seasonings.

To cure the cod — Whisk together the sugar, salt, and aromatics, ensuring they are well combined. Spread half the cure over the bottom of a small baking sheet. Put the fish on top and cover with the remaining cure. Set aside for 20 to 30 minutes at room temperature. It's worth checking sooner than you expect, rather than overcuring it; it should feel tighter and firmer. Rinse off the cure and pat dry with paper towels.

To make the cod broth — Heat the olive oil in a pan over medium heat. Add the cod trimmings, garlic, and 1 quart/1 L water, then simmer gently for 20 to 30 minutes. Remove from the heat, cover, and leave to infuse for another 30 minutes.

To make the açorda — Heat the olive oil in a pan over low heat. Add the garlic and cilantro stalks and cook gently for 5 minutes, until soft and fragrant. Season with salt and pepper. Pour in the cod broth and bring to a boil over high heat. Reduce the heat to low, add the cured cod, and poach for 5 minutes, until just starting to flake gently apart. Stir in the cilantro leaves and taste for seasoning. Toast the bread. To serve, place a slice of toast in each bowl with a few mint leaves on top. Spoon the cod and broth over the toast, adding a little more broth than you think you need, as the bread will absorb a lot. Drizzle with extra-virgin olive oil and serve.

Octopus with smashed potatoes, olive oil, and piso *Polvo à lagareiro com batata a murro*

Serves 4 to 6

For the octopus

1 octopus (about 21 ounces/600 g), cleaned, with head, eyes, and innards removed

2 bay leaves

1 white onion, quartered

2 garlic cloves

Flaky sea salt and ground white pepper

For the piso

A bunch of cilantro, leaves and stalks finely chopped

½ garlic clove, finely crushed

Finely grated zest of ½ lemon, plus freshly squeezed juice (optional)

Flaky sea salt and ground white pepper

3 tablespoons extra-virgin olive oil, plus extra for drizzling

For the smashed potatoes

8 to 12 potatoes, such as Yukon gold, skin on

4 tablespoons olive oil

2 bay leaves

4 garlic cloves, smashed

Flaky sea salt and ground white pepper

This dish is smothered in fragrant green extra-virgin olive oil, hence the name: a *lagareiro* is the owner of an olive oil press. The smell reminds me of summer days on the beaches outside Lisbon, when the scent of grilled octopus wafts alluringly through the air. Perfectly crisp octopus, caramelized around the edges, is unbelievably good—especially when served with twice-cooked potatoes and the delicious Portuguese herb-and-oil condiment *piso*. This varies from region to region, even person to person, and you can add any combination of herbs and citrus, even almonds and chile, depending on what it's to go with—let your imagination run wild. I like to make a double, triple, or quadruple batch and store it in the fridge for a week. It works well as a marinade too.

To cook the octopus — Rinse the octopus under cold running water. Half-fill a large pan with water and add the bay leaves, onion, and garlic and a generous pinch of salt and pepper. Bring to a boil, add the octopus, and boil for 3 minutes. Carefully remove the octopus and set it aside to rest for a few minutes. Bring the same water to a boil again and repeat the process two more times. In this way you can control the cooking process and check how firm the octopus flesh is becoming. At this point, the flesh should be tender with a little resistance when you insert a knife, and the skin will feel slightly gelatinous.

Turn the heat down to low. Simmer the octopus, covered, for 20 minutes. Remove it from the pan and allow it to cool. If you have time, chill it overnight, which allows the flesh to become firmer. When the octopus has cooled, cut it into 1½-inch/3 to 4-cm pieces.

To make the piso — Mix together the cilantro, garlic, and lemon zest with a generous pinch of salt and pepper until you have a paste. I like to make this in a mortar and pestle, but you can also chop everything very finely by hand. By adding salt at this early stage, the flavor will be drawn out from the garlic. Stir in the olive oil. I like it sharp, and I add about 2 tablespoons lemon juice just before serving so it doesn't discolor. It will keep in the fridge for a few days with an extra glug of olive oil on top. →

→ *To make the smashed potatoes* — Preheat the oven to 410°F/210°C (convection 375°F/190°C). Cook the potatoes in plenty of salted boiling water until just tender but not breaking up. Remove from the pan, drain well, and leave until cool enough to handle. *Murro* means "punch" in Portuguese, and we are now going to punch the potatoes. Smash each one gently with the palm of your hand. Toss them in a bowl with the olive oil, bay leaves, and garlic, and season with salt and pepper. Put them in a large baking dish (big enough to hold the octopus too) and bake for 30 minutes, or until golden brown and crispy.

Drizzle the octopus with extra-virgin olive oil and put the pieces on top of the potatoes. Increase the oven temperature to 430°F/220°C (convection 390°F/200°C) and cook for 10 minutes, or until the octopus has lovely crispy edges. Drizzle with the *piso*, take it straight to the table, and let your guests help themselves.

Grilled sea bass with fennel and kale

Robalo de mar grelhado com funcho e couve galega

Serves 2

5 tablespoons olive oil,
    plus extra for drizzling
1 white onion, thinly sliced
2 garlic cloves, crushed
1 fennel bulb, trimmed and thinly sliced
1 small long red chile, seeded
    and thinly sliced
2 strips lemon zest, finely chopped
1 whole sea bass, gutted and butterflied
A large handful of parsley leaves,
    finely chopped
Flaky sea salt and ground white pepper
1 tablespoon red wine vinegar
7 ounces/200 g green kale
A large handful of cilantro leaves,
    finely chopped

In Lisbon, where you can find amazing-quality sea bass, it's unusual to serve the fish off the bone, as it is here. This is a wonderful way to show off the robust flavor of the fish, however; ask your fishmonger to butterfly the sea bass (in other words, to scale, gut, and bone it, leaving the fillets attached along the top), then get creative with the stuffing. I've used fennel and kale here, but you can experiment with *chouriço*, lemon, *piso*, cilantro, bay leaf, blood sausage— whatever takes your fancy.

First, make the stuffing. Heat 2 tablespoons of the oil in a frying pan over low heat, add the onion, garlic, and fennel, and cook gently for 10 minutes, or until soft. Add the chile and lemon zest and cook for another 5 minutes, then remove from the heat and set the stuffing aside in a bowl.

Preheat the broiler to high. Make three diagonal slashes in the skin on both sides of the fish. Rub half the stuffing into the cavities of the fish, then close it up again. Drizzle the skin with oil and sprinkle half the parsley over it, then season with salt and pepper. Broil for 20 minutes, or until cooked through and crisp. If the skin takes on too much color before the inside is cooked, cover it with foil.

Heat the remaining 3 tablespoons/45 ml olive oil in the frying pan over medium heat and add the rest of the stuffing, along with the red wine vinegar. Add the kale and cook for 3 to 4 minutes. Remove the pan from the heat and stir in the remaining parsley and the cilantro, then serve immediately. I like to take the whole sea bass to the table with the kale spooned on top, along with all the beautiful juices from the pan.

Confit cod, egg, and chickpea
salad *Meia desfeita*

Serves 4

For the confit cod
2 cups/500 ml extra-virgin olive oil
1 bay leaf
1 garlic clove, smashed
½ long red chile, cut into chunks
4 (5-ounce/150 g) cured cod fillets
    (page 97)

For the chickpeas
14 ounces/400 g dried chickpeas, soaked
    overnight with water to cover and a
    pinch of baking soda
1 shallot, halved
1 carrot, halved
1 stalk celery, cut into chunks
1 bay leaf
1 garlic clove, halved
1¾ ounces/50 g ham hock or
    smoked bacon, in one piece (optional)
Flaky sea salt and ground white pepper

For the salad
4 eggs
A small bunch of cilantro, leaves picked
A small bunch of parsley, leaves picked
1 red onion, finely chopped
Freshly squeezed juice of 2 lemons
3 tablespoons/40 ml Chardonnay vinegar or
    other good-quality white wine vinegar
6 tablespoons extra-virgin olive oil,
    plus extra to garnish
Flaky sea salt and ground white pepper
Smoked paprika

Meia desfeita is a typical city workers' lunch, which used to be made using salt cod trimmings rather than the whole fish, bulked up with chickpeas and a boiled egg. It is a delicious dish, and the fact that here the fish is not the main event, playing instead a complementary role, reminds me a little of Japanese cuisine. A plateful of this nourishing dish will give you the energy to get through the afternoon, whatever you're going to be doing. Some grilled bread on the side would be lovely.

To make the confit cod — Put all the ingredients except the cod in a medium pan and gently heat to 185°F/85°C, or when the oil just starts to bubble (take care that it does not boil). Remove from the heat, wait for 5 minutes, then slide in the cod and leave it in the oil as it cools. After 15 minutes it should be cooked through and flaking nicely. Remove and carefully transfer to a plate, then gently break it apart into bite-size chunks.

To cook the chickpeas — Drain and rinse the chickpeas, put them in a pan, and cover with cold water, adding the shallot, carrot, celery, bay leaf, garlic, and ham hock. Bring to a boil, then simmer gently for 45 minutes to 1 hour, or until soft. Remove the pan from the heat, season with salt and pepper, and leave to cool in the cooking liquid.

To make the salad — Lower the eggs into a pan of boiling salted water and gently simmer for 6 minutes. Remove from the pan and put them in iced water to stop them cooking. Once cool, peel the eggs. Finely chop most of the herbs, reserving a few whole leaves to garnish, if you like.

Drain the chickpeas and put them in a bowl with all the salad ingredients except the eggs. Season with salt, pepper, and paprika and mix well. Spoon the salad onto a large serving plate and scatter the chunks of cod over the top. Cut the eggs in half and place them on top with the reserved parsley and cilantro leaves, if using, then drizzle with extra-virgin olive oil.

Fish soup
Sopa de peixe

Serves 4

For the fish stock
3 tablespoons olive oil
1 onion, coarsely chopped
1 fennel bulb, coarsely chopped
2 carrots, coarsely chopped
2 garlic cloves, smashed
1 bay leaf
10 ounces/300 g fish trimmings
4 ripe plum tomatoes, roughly chopped
3 tablespoons/50 ml white wine
Flaky sea salt and ground white pepper

For the soup
3 tablespoons olive oil
2 onions, finely chopped
1 bay leaf
Flaky sea salt and ground white pepper
2 garlic cloves, crushed
A small bunch of cilantro, stalks
     finely chopped and leaves picked
Smoked paprika
6 ripe plum tomatoes, coarsely chopped
¼ cup/60 ml white wine
1½ ounces/40 g small pasta, such as elbow
     macaroni or shells
10 ounces/300 g fish fillet (see headnote),
     cut into bite-size pieces
17 ounces/500 g deveined, shell-on shrimp
     or cleaned live mussels or clams

To serve
4 slices sourdough bread
1 garlic clove, halved
Finely grated zest of 1 lemon
A small handful of parsley leaves,
     coarsely chopped
Extra-virgin olive oil

There is a fantastic abundance of fish and seafood in Portugal, so our fish soups are complex in flavor and incredibly diverse in texture. We often add small elbow macaroni pasta, which absorbs the flavors from the stock and brings an extra dimension to the dish. Go to town with the varieties of fish and seafood you use (try red mullet, sea bass, bream, mackerel, or pollock), and be sure to ask for the trimmings from your fishmonger, as they make for a better broth. This will not be a clear soup, but one with deep flavor.

To make the fish stock — Heat the oil in a large deep pan over low heat. Add the onion, fennel, and carrots and cook gently for 10 minutes. Add the garlic, bay leaf, and fish trimmings and cook for a few more minutes, then add the tomatoes, increase the heat, and cook until they have lightly caramelized. Pour in 1 quart/1 L of water and the white wine and bring to a boil over high heat, then reduce the heat and simmer gently for 25 to 30 minutes. Skim off any scum that rises to the surface.

When the stock is ready, remove it from the heat, cover, and leave it to infuse for 20 minutes, then strain it. Season lightly with salt and pepper. This is a very versatile stock; you could use it for the Shrimp and Shellfish Rice (page 199), in fish stews, or to poach white fish such as halibut or sea bass.

To make the soup — Heat the oil in a large, wide pan over low heat. Add the onions and bay leaf and cook for 5 minutes, seasoning with salt and pepper. Add the garlic, cilantro stalks, and paprika to taste, and cook for a few minutes more. When the onions are translucent, add the tomatoes. Increase the heat to medium and cook until the vegetables start to lightly caramelize. Pour in the wine and cook briefly, then add 1 quart/1 L of fish stock and simmer for 10 minutes. Add the pasta and simmer for 2 minutes (you don't want to cook it all the way through at this stage), then taste for seasoning, remembering that the seafood is salty.

Add the fish and poach it in the soup for 1 to 2 minutes, then add the shrimp, mussels, or clams and stir well. Cook for another 2 to 3 minutes, then cover, shake the pan, and remove it from the heat. Leave it to sit for a few minutes.

To serve — Toast the bread and rub each slice with the cut garlic. Bring the soup pan to the table and open the lid to breathe in its wonderful fragrances. Discard any unopened shellfish. Sprinkle on the lemon zest, cilantro and parsley leaves, and a generous drizzle of extra-virgin olive oil. A little more paprika would be lovely too. Pour the soup over the toasts to serve.

Grilled sardines with green peppers
Sardinhas assadas com salada de pimentos

Serves 2

1 sweet onion, thinly sliced

Flaky sea salt and ground white pepper

A small bunch of cilantro, leaves
finely chopped and stalks reserved

A small bunch of parsley, leaves
finely chopped

Finely grated zest of ½ lemon

3 tablespoons extra-virgin olive oil,
plus extra for brushing

2 green peppers

2 teaspoons white wine vinegar

4 large, plump sardines, butterflied,
backbone removed, and pinboned

4 bay leaves

4 strips lemon zest

4 strips lime zest

Toasted bread, to serve

When I tried to cook this sardine dish recently, the first thing I did was put the prepared fish next to the grill—which happened to be on a roof terrace in downtown Lisbon—before turning my back for a minute. Big mistake. I must warn you: don't leave your sparkling-fresh sardines outside unattended, for the seagulls will get them. The thought of those greedy birds flying away with my beautiful fish still makes me laugh.

Sardines are always cooked whole in Lisbon, but because of a rather unfortunate childhood encounter with a fish bone I prefer to remove the bones, which is a kind of sacrilege, but what can I say? Here, the sardine bellies are stuffed with lemon zest and bay leaves, and are delicious alongside grilled green peppers and a slice of toasted sourdough to soak up the juices.

Put the onion in a small bowl with a pinch of sea salt, add water to cover, and leave to soak for a few minutes. (This will break the onion down a little so that the flavor is not as strong.)

Mix together the cilantro and parsley leaves and lemon zest with a generous pinch of salt and white pepper. Stir in the extra-virgin olive oil until you have a paste.

Preheat the broiler to high, then broil the peppers until the skin is blackened all over, turning them a couple of times. Transfer to a container and cover tightly with plastic wrap. Once cooled, peel, seed, and thinly slice the peppers. Drain the onions and mix them with the peppers, white wine vinegar, and a few tablespoons of the herb paste. Leave to marinate until you are ready to serve.

Gently open the sardines and stuff them with the bay leaves, lemon and lime zest, and chopped cilantro stalks, and season well with salt and pepper. Brush the skin with olive oil and sprinkle with salt. Grill for about 3 to 4 minutes, or until crisp on the outside and cooked through. Spoon some of the herb paste onto the toasted bread and top with a sardine, then add more paste. Serve the peppers on the side.

Baked salt cod with caramelized onions and potatoes *Bacalhau à Gomes de Sá*

Serves 4

14 ounces/400 g potatoes, such as
    Yukon gold or similar
3 tablespoons olive oil, plus
    extra for drizzling
4 onions, thinly sliced
Flaky sea salt and ground white pepper
2 garlic cloves, finely chopped,
    plus 1 halved garlic clove
10 ounces/300 g cured cod (page 97,
    but cure it for only 20 minutes)
3 eggs
A small handful of black olives,
    sliced into rings
A handful of parsley leaves, finely chopped
Extra-virgin olive oil, to serve

There are at least 365 salt cod recipes in Portuguese cuisine, one for every day of the year, but this is one of the few that everyone knows. *Bacalhau à Gomes de Sá* was created in a restaurant in Porto, where the chef, after whom the dish is named, was the son of a cod merchant who had gone bankrupt. He apparently said, "If you change anything in this recipe, it won't be good," but I have to say I don't agree with him. I have replaced dried salt cod with freshly cured cod, which makes the dish creamy rather than salty. Make sure the onions are caramelized slowly, to bring out their sweetness.

Preheat the oven to 410°F/210°C (convection 375°F/190°C). Cook the potatoes in boiling salted water until soft but not mushy, then drain. Once cool enough to handle, cut horizontally into ⅓-inch/1-cm slices.

Heat the olive oil in a pan over medium heat. Add the onions and cook gently for 10 minutes, until soft, and season well with salt and pepper. Add the chopped garlic and cook until fragrant. Increase the heat slightly to caramelize the onions, stirring well to ensure they don't stick. Once they are caramelized and sweet, remove the pan from the heat.

Oil the bottom of a large ovenproof baking dish and rub it with the halved garlic clove. Cut the cod into bite-size chunks. Make an even layer of potatoes on the bottom of the dish, then one of onions, followed by one of cod. Repeat with another layer of each and finish with a layer of potatoes and onions. Cover with a lid or foil and bake for 25 minutes, or until golden brown and cooked through, removing the lid after 10 minutes.

Put the eggs in a pan of cold water, ensuring they are fully covered. Bring the water to a boil over high heat, then remove the pan from the heat, cover, and leave for 10 minutes. Put the eggs in iced water to stop the cooking and peel them once cool.

Just before serving, slice the eggs into wedges. Scatter the eggs, olives, and parsley on top of the potatoes and onions. Serve hot, straight from the baking dish, with a drizzle of extra-virgin olive oil.

Shrimp bread porridge
Açorda de gambas

Serves 2

10 ounces/300 g large fresh shrimp,
    shell and head on
5 tablespoons olive oil
7 ounces/200 g sourdough or ciabatta
1 fresh corn on the cob
1 small fennel bulb, trimmed and
    thinly sliced
2 garlic cloves, crushed
3½ ounces/100 g ripe tomatoes,
    coarsely chopped
A small handful of cilantro, stalks
    and leaves chopped separately
3 whole egg yolks
Flaky sea salt and ground white pepper
Worcestershire sauce (optional)
Freshly squeezed lemon juice
Extra-virgin olive oil, to serve

Shrimp *açorda*, a kind of bread-thickened soup, is dreamy when made well. I like mine spiced and lemony, bound together with a flavorful stock made from the shells of the shrimp. If you can get your hands on some really good sweet red Carabineros shrimp, use only the shells for the stock and add the flesh right at the end, so that it's almost raw and just heated through. Some of the *marisqueiras* (shellfish restaurants) around Guincho beach west of Lisbon serve fabulous *açordas*, and it's just perfect to eat this by the sea.

Bring a large pan of water to a boil and add the shrimp. Boil for 3 to 4 minutes, or until the shells turn pink. Remove the shrimp, reserving the cooking water. Once cool enough to handle, twist the heads to remove them. Peel them and use a small knife to make a slit along the middle of the back of each one, then pull out the veins.

Heat 2 tablespoons of the olive oil in a large pan over medium heat, add the shrimp shells and heads, and cook for a few minutes to release their flavor. Cover with the reserved cooking water and simmer gently for 20 minutes. Strain, reserving the liquid and discarding the shells. Tear the bread into rough chunks. Pour 2 cups/500 ml of shrimp stock over the bread and leave to soak in a bowl for 20 minutes.

Preheat the broiler to medium-high, add the corn, and broil for 10 to 12 minutes, until just golden brown and crispy, turning it halfway during cooking. Once cooled slightly, cut the kernels off the cob.

Heat the remaining 3 tablespoons olive oil in a pan over low heat. Add the fennel and cook gently for 10 minutes, or until soft, then add the garlic and cook until fragrant. Pour in the soaked bread and add the tomatoes, cilantro stalks, and corn. Cook over low heat for 5 minutes, then stir in the shrimp and 1 egg yolk. Taste for seasoning and add a dash of Worcestershire sauce.

Serve in bowls with a fresh egg yolk on top of each one, and add a good squeeze of lemon juice, some extra-virgin olive oil, and the cilantro leaves.

Monkfish and chouriço cataplana
Cataplana de tamboril

Serves 4

7 ounces/200 g waxy fingerling potatoes,
    such as La Reine

4 tablespoons olive oil

2 onions, thinly sliced

Flaky sea salt and ground white pepper

2 garlic cloves, crushed

5 ounces/150 g chouriço (skin removed),
    finely chopped

8 plum tomatoes, finely chopped

3 tablespoons/50 ml light cream

7 tablespoons/100 ml dry white wine

17 ounces/500 g monkfish, cut into
    thin medallions

20 large clams, purged and scrubbed

A small handful of parsley leaves,
    finely chopped

A *cataplana* is a large copper-colored metal cooking vessel made from two domes hinged together, resembling a clam. Introduced to Portugal by the Moors, it gently steams fish, meat, or vegetables to create a fragrant stew with stock that's full of flavor. Unlike most restaurants, I parcook some of the ingredients first so that the monkfish and potatoes will be perfectly cooked, and not overdone. If you can't find a *cataplana* you could use a wide, shallow pan with a lid instead—just make sure you resist the temptation to open it before the cooking time is up.

Cut the potatoes in half, keeping any smaller ones whole. Cook them in plenty of boiling salted water for 8 to 10 minutes, or until just soft but not mushy. Drain and set aside.

Heat the olive oil in a *cataplana* or wide, shallow pan over low heat. Add the onions and cook gently for about 10 minutes, or until soft and juicy, then season with salt and pepper. Add the garlic and cook until fragrant, then add the *chouriço* and cook until the edges are crisp.

Pour in the tomatoes, cream, wine, and 3 or 4 tablespoons/ 50 ml of water and simmer for 1 to 2 minutes. Add a little more water if it seems too dry. Stir in the monkfish and clams, cover with a lid, and shake the pan. After 2 minutes, take the pan off the heat and discard any unopened clams. Taste for seasoning, stir in the parsley, and serve immediately.

Sausage and cabbage rolls with tomato sauce *Salsichas com couve lombarda*

Serves 4

3 tablespoons olive oil

2 onions, thinly sliced

Flaky sea salt and ground white pepper

2 garlic cloves, crushed

1 bay leaf

3 thin slices bacon

14 ounces/400 g canned chopped tomatoes

⅓ cup/80 ml dry white wine

1 Savoy cabbage, leaves separated
    and hard stem removed

8 to 12 good-quality pork sausages

3 slices sourdough or ciabatta bread

This is a canteen dish at heart—my father used to work for a large pharmaceutical company and sometimes I would join him at lunchtime just to eat this. With great ingredients, it has become a classic of the Portuguese repertoire. Make sure you use the best-quality sausages you can find, with a high pork content, perhaps from an Italian deli or your butcher. Go for the plainest ones possible, with nothing more than seasoning added. It's worth making the sauce base ahead of time, so that you can let it rest long enough for the flavors to develop nicely.

Preheat the oven to 375°F/190°C (convection 340°F/170°C). Heat 2 tablespoons of the olive oil in a pan over medium heat. Add the onions and cook gently for 10 minutes, or until soft and juicy. Season well with salt and pepper. Add the garlic, bay leaf, and bacon and cook for 5 minutes. Pour in the tomatoes, increase the heat, and cook for 5 minutes, or until the tomatoes have sizzled and reduced. Stir in the white wine, reduce the heat to low, and simmer for 20 minutes.

Meanwhile, blanch the cabbage in a large pan of boiling salted water for 3 minutes. Remove and cool in iced water to stop the cooking. Using the greenest leaves, wrap each sausage in a cabbage leaf and secure with a toothpick.

Taste the sauce for seasoning, then pour most of it into a large baking dish. Arrange the cabbage rolls in the sauce, then spoon over the remaining sauce. Cover with foil and bake for 25 minutes, or until cooked through. After 10 minutes of cooking, remove the foil.

Meanwhile, drizzle the bread with the remaining olive oil and season well with salt and pepper. Bake for 5 minutes, or until golden brown, then leave to cool and chop into rough breadcrumbs. To serve, remove the toothpicks from the cabbage-sausage rolls and sprinkle the breadcrumbs on top.

Roasted orange-rubbed pork belly
with fennel *Barriga de porco assada com laranja*

Serves 4

For the marinade
5 garlic cloves, crushed
2 teaspoons flaky sea salt
1 teaspoon ground white pepper
2 teaspoons smoked paprika
A small bunch of cilantro,
    leaves and stalks finely chopped
1 long red chile, seeded and
    finely chopped
Juice and finely grated zest
    of 1 orange
4 tablespoons olive oil

For the pork
1¾ pounds/800 g boneless pork belly
1 fennel bulb
2 sweet onions
3 tablespoons/40 ml dry white wine

I first made this dish when I invited some Portuguese friends to celebrate Christmas with me at my first restaurant in London. Because the restaurant was closed, we used the open kitchen to cook in and set up a long table in the middle of the dining room. We ate, drank, opened presents, and celebrated into the wee hours of the morning of December 25—just as in Portugal, where the real party is on Christmas Eve. This may not be a traditional dish, but it is a delicious one: the skin is crisp and the insides are lovely and succulent, flavored with the unmistakably Portuguese notes of orange and cilantro.

To marinate the pork — Using an immersion blender or small food processor, blend together all the ingredients for the marinade. With a sharp, pointed knife, score the skin of the pork belly all over in a crisscross pattern. Rub the marinade all over the belly and leave to marinate for a couple of hours in the fridge, or ideally overnight.

To cook the pork — Preheat the oven to 320°F/160°C (convection 285°F/140°C). Slice the fennel and onions into roughly equal pieces, put them in a baking dish, and put the pork belly on top with its marinade. Pour in the white wine. Roast the pork belly for 2½ hours, or until tender all the way through. Increase the oven temperature to 410°F/210°C (convection 375°F/190°C) and roast for another 10 minutes, or until the skin is crisp. Remove from the oven and leave to rest on a warm plate. Cut into thin slices, making sure everyone gets a piece of the lovely crackling. Serve with the fennel and onions on the side.

Tascas

For much of Lisbon's population, tascas are the heart and soul of social life. They are small restaurants, a bit like a local pub, which many locals visit nearly every day. Almost everyone is loyal to their favorite tasca, and for legions of *lisboetas* it's a kind of second home—they'll come in on their own but sit down at a table and eat with other regulars, just like a family. Some—particularly older people—will arrive clutching plastic Tupperware boxes and take the food back home to eat. In one *tasca*, Casa Cid, I remember watching as the waiter untied a bib from a customer's neck and removed it for him. There was a touching paternal intimacy about it that confirmed my belief that these places are as much about personal relationships as they are about the cooking—this is service, old style.

Every day there are specials, such as *cozido à portuguesa* (a meat and vegetable stew; *cozido* simply means "cooked") and *feijoada* (a bean and meat stew), more often than not served in enormous portions on an oval metal platter. Both of these are authentically rustic and contain many cuts of meat, including bones, so don't be surprised to find pigs' ears and bits of cartilage if you order them. The specials of the day will be written in marker pen on paper tablecloths and pinned up outside. The quality of the food varies, of course, but there are some truly excellent *tascas*, and what they all have in common is that they're cheap: you can have bread, a starter, a main course, a dessert, and a glass of inexpensive (sometimes rough!) wine for less than fifteen euros. Some *tascas* are known for a particular special that creates a cult following and a line right out the door—if you hear of one, make sure you get there well before one o'clock or you'll have little chance of getting in. Squeeze in beside the people in suits, hi-vis building site jackets, and hipster beards.

Often small and roughly decorated, *tascas* usually have zinc on the bar, strip lights on the ceiling, and sometimes a "feature" sink in the wall for hand-washing right in the middle of the dining room. In Lisbon, many *tascas* are tribal, and profess their love of the local football team Benfica or its rival, Sporting, by hanging dozens of football scarves on the wall. At Stop do Bairro in Campo de Ourique there are football shirts, flags, and scarves everywhere, and the food is great. The name means "neighborhood stop," which sums up what a *tasca* is. The tables are crammed together, but that just means you can see what other people are eating, which makes ordering that much easier. Like any truly terrific *tasca*, they cook amazing fries from good baking potatoes in hot oil, always with a beautiful yellow color. I loved their version of *toucinho do céu*, an almond cake whose name literally means "bacon of heaven." The best *tascas* are always a bit of a trek from the central touristy area of historic Lisbon and this one is no exception, but it's worth it.

Venture into some of the old districts like Mouraria or Alcântara and you'll find *tascas* with grit, character, and history. In Graça, on top of Lisbon's highest hill, I was allowed into the tiny kitchen at O Cardoso do Estrela de Ouro early one morning to see the two women cooks prepare for the very long day ahead. Dona Laura Cardoso uses a traditional electric branding iron to caramelize the top of her *leite creme*—Portuguese crème brûlée— while keeping her eye on vast bubbling pots and frying some of the best *croquetes de carne* (meat croquettes) I've tasted in Lisbon. She's helped by Dona Emilia, who hails from Minho in the north, and always sings while she works. Like most women in *tasca* kitchens, their hair is scooped up in a hat with a net at the back. Front of house, Senhor Cardoso scuttles between the tables, the kitchen, the bar, and the *montra* (window display), bringing fish to show the customers. At midday, just before the lunchtime rush, they all sit down together at a table and eat, often joined by a few late-morning regulars.

Tascas began life as charcoal shops (*carvoaria*) in the days when charcoal was the main fuel used in the city because it was easily transported up and down the coast and rivers. Senhor Cardoso explains this to me with a laugh: "The person who was going to carry charcoal needed wine before humping it on their back—then they started offering *salgadinhos* (small savory snacks) to go with the wine. And then, in the 1980s, when *tascas* stopped selling charcoal, we expanded into lunch and dinner."

From late spring onward the *tascas* sell *caracóis* (small snails). We start eating them on May 1, in celebration of Labor Day, and from then until

Estamos na
MADRAGOA
Aqui bebe-se
a melhor Ginja
de Lisboa
Ginja Ribeira
Nova (cada shot)· 1,50€

SEJA BRANCO OU SEJA TINTO
NÃO IMPORTA A COR QUE ELE TEM,
BEBIDO AQUI NESTA CASA
TODO ELE SABE BEM!

about September you'll see handwritten signs all over the city proclaiming *Há caracóis!*—We have snails! These are not like French escargots at all; they're much smaller and much cheaper—they're peasant food, in essence, that came to the city and started a craze. *Lisboetas* love to sit with a cold beer—the glass must come from the fridge—and a plate piled with the things, poking them with pins until the meat comes out. Snails might freak you out, but they're fun to eat—if you feel shy order a *pires* (small plate), or go full-on Portuguese and get a *travessa* (big plate). *Caracóis* are cooked in a spicy, salty broth scented with oregano, chile, garlic, bay leaf, white pepper, and sometimes cilantro, and they absorb all of this so that each snail becomes a little umami bomb of flavor. I love to mop up the juices with a chunk of good bread. We also enjoy eating *tremoços* (lupini beans) with our beer. Like the snails, the beans are cooked in a salty brine. You break the shell like a fava bean, with your teeth, and you squeeze the yellow seed inside it into your mouth.

Many *tascas*—particularly those in the Alfama and Mouraria districts—are associated with fado, the maudlin Portuguese style of music that began around 1820 and is still popular today. It's melancholic folk music, usually sung by a solo artist accompanied by guitar. I'm not much of a fan, if I'm being honest, because I think our country was a sad place for too long and I don't like to be reminded of it by these songs, which are almost always complaining. Many of my fellow *lisboetas* and our visitors love it, though. To me, *tascas* are a celebration of food and community, so you'll find me in a rustic one—one without the fado, with people chatting and laughing and loving just being together—with an icy cold *imperial* (beer) and a plate of goodness in front of me.

Roast kid goat
Cabrito assado no forno

Serves 4

For the marinade
2 tablespoons smoked paprika
1 tablespoon flaky sea salt
2 teaspoons ground white pepper
4 garlic cloves, crushed
⅞ cup/200 ml white wine
2 tablespoons olive oil
2 tablespoons red pepper paste
    (page 173)

For the goat
2½ pounds/1.2 kg kid goat shoulder
4 bay leaves
6 yellow potatoes, such as Yukon gold
    or similar, cut into thick chunks
3 white onions, cut into thick chunks
6 carrots, cut into thick chunks
5 garlic cloves, smashed
6 tablespoons/75 g cold butter, diced

Kid goat is a highly regarded meat in Portugal, both out of necessity—it makes sense to eat the young male goats that cannot produce milk—and for its unique flavor, which is stronger than that of milk-producing animals. It is becoming increasingly available in other countries, but if you can't find it, older lamb would also work well. This recipe was designed for a home oven, but if you're lucky enough to have a wood-fired pizza oven in your garden, this is a great opportunity to make the most of it. It's well worth tracking down or making some *massa de pimentão* (red pepper paste; page 173); its characteristic flavor would be hard to replace.

To marinate the goat — Using an immersion blender or small food processor, blend all the marinade ingredients into a purée. Pour the marinade over the goat and rub it into the flesh. Put 2 bay leaves under the goat and 2 on the skin. Marinate overnight, or ideally for 2 days, in the fridge, turning it once.

To cook the goat — Preheat the oven to 320°F/160°C (convection 285°F/140°C). Put the vegetables in a baking dish large enough to fit all the vegetables and goat but still be quite snug. Sit the goat on top of the vegetables. Add a splash of water to the marinade left in the marinating dish and pour this all over the goat, taking care to get all the juices. Dot the butter on top and cover loosely with foil. Bake for 2 hours, then remove the foil and bake for another hour. Increase the heat to 390°F/200°C (convection 355°F/180°C) for the last 10 minutes to crisp up the skin.

Café-style steak
Bife à café

Serves 2

2 (6-ounce/180 g) sirloin steaks
Flaky sea salt and cracked black pepper
2 tablespoons olive oil
A knob of butter
1 small shallot, finely diced
1 tablespoon brandy
1 tablespoon Madeira
1 teaspoon Portuguese-style mustard
   (see page 20)
¼ cup/60 ml light cream
Worcestershire sauce
2 slices Ibérico ham

Bife à café, a real Lisbon favorite, takes its name from Café Marrare in the Chiado area, a coffee club frequented by the city's poets and intellectuals, and also famous for its steak. Thanks to the name, some people imagine that the sauce contains coffee, but traditionally it's more of a creamy pepper sauce. Using good-quality meat will add hugely to this dish; I like a nice dry-aged sirloin steak. Finish it off with a slice of cured ham or a fried egg on top, as the Portuguese do. Eat it with fried potatoes and some piri piri oil (page 156) or Tabasco, if you like.

Take the steaks out of the fridge at least 20 minutes before cooking and season them well on both sides with salt and pepper. Heat the olive oil in a frying pan over high heat. When the pan is very hot, add the steaks and cook for 2 to 3 minutes on each side for medium-rare (the exact cooking time will depend on the thickness of the steaks). Add the butter and baste the steaks with it. Remove the steaks and leave to rest on a warm plate.

Add the shallot to the cooking juices in the pan and cook over low heat until soft, then increase the heat to caramelize it. Pour in the brandy and Madeira and stir quickly to incorporate all the cooking juices and sediment. Add the mustard and cream and cook for another couple of minutes.

Taste for seasoning and add some more salt, pepper, and Worcestershire sauce, if you like. If the sauce is a little thick or starting to separate, add a dash of warm water. Put a slice of ham on each steak, pour the sauce on top, and eat right away.

→ You are looking for the consistency of loose porridge. Once cooked, remove the chicken, bay leaves, and cinnamon. When the chicken has cooled slightly, pull the meat off the bones, coarsely chop it, then return it to the pan. Season with salt, pepper, and lemon juice. I also like to add a little extra Ibérico pork fat or duck fat.

To make the piso — Mix together the cilantro leaves (reserving a few to garnish), garlic, and lemon zest with a generous pinch of salt and pepper to make a paste. Stir in the olive oil.

To serve — Ladle the soup into bowls, drizzle over the *piso* and olive oil generously, and sprinkle with the reserved cilantro leaves.

Grilled piri piri chicken with potato chips *Frango na brasa com piri piri*

Serves 4

1 (3¼-pound/1.6 kg) whole chicken

Flaky sea salt and ground white pepper

2 bay leaves

3 tablespoons/40 g butter

1 tablespoon brandy

A large handful of parsley leaves,
    finely chopped

For the piri piri paste

6 garlic cloves, crushed

1 long red chile, thinly sliced

1 lemon, coarsely diced

6 tablespoons olive oil

Flaky sea salt and cracked black pepper

For the potato chips

3 medium potatoes, such as Yukon golds

Vegetable oil, for frying

Your choice of chopped herbs,
    flavored salts, and oils (optional)

You'll no doubt have heard of piri piri chicken, as it features on the menu of several international restaurant chains. Their reinvention of the dish has nothing on the real thing, which is spatchcocked and cooked slowly over charcoal, constantly basted with hot, fragrant butter. It originated in Mozambique, a former Portuguese colony, where the fiery piri piri or *malagueta* chiles were grown. If you cook it on a wood-fired grill, you might be transported to this far-away tropical place—but you can also roast it in the oven!

Freshly fried potato chips are eaten throughout Portugal as a snack, or to accompany sandwiches and rotisserie chicken. Traditionally, the chips are served salted, but there are many other flavoring options you can try. You can use salts, herbs, and chile oils to enhance your chips—the sky really is the limit in terms of the seasoning.

Spatchcock the chicken, or ask your butcher to do it for you. This involves removing the backbone so that the chicken can be completely flattened out, ensuring even and quick cooking. Put the chicken breast-side down on a board, its legs facing toward you. With strong kitchen scissors, cut along both sides of the backbone from the tail to the head to remove it. Spread the chicken out and turn it over, then press down on the breastbone firmly until you have flattened it. Make a few diagonal slashes along the breast on each side. Season the skin generously with salt and pepper and chill for 2 hours. This draws out moisture for increased flavor and makes the skin crisper during cooking.

To make the piri piri paste — Pound the garlic, chile, lemon, and olive oil with sea salt and white pepper in a mortar and pestle or purée them with an immersion blender or small food processor. Rub the paste all over the chicken skin and leave to marinate for another 2 hours, if you have time.

To make the potato chips — Peel the potatoes and slice them as thinly as you can, using a mandoline. Rinse them under cold water to remove excess starch so that they don't color too quickly when frying. Pat them dry with paper towels, then put the slices in a clean kitchen towel and carefully wring it out →

→ to squeeze out all the moisture. Fill a large, heavy-bottomed pan one-third full with oil and heat it to 310°F/165°C. Fry the potatoes in small batches for 3 to 5 minutes, or until cooked but still pale. Remove the chips with a slotted spoon and increase the oil temperature to 355°F/180°C. Fry the chips again briefly in batches until golden and crispy. (Do not overcrowd the pan, and take care that the oil temperature does not rise too high.) Use a slotted spoon to remove them from the pan and drain on paper towels, then sprinkle with salt and pepper and whatever flavorings you wish to use.

To cook the chicken — Preheat the oven to 430°F/220°C (convection 390°F/200°C). Put the bay leaves on a baking sheet and place the chicken on top. Roast for 45 minutes to 1 hour, or until cooked through, basting regularly. Remove and transfer to a warm plate to rest for about 15 minutes. Pour all the cooking juices from the dish into a pan, including the lovely fat. Warm the juices, adding the butter and brandy. Simmer gently for 1 to 2 minutes, then remove from the heat and stir in the parsley. Pour over the chicken and serve immediately with the chips.

Slow-simmered bean, cabbage, and pork stew *Feijoada*

Serves 4

For the beans

6 ounces/180 g dried beans (I like to
   use a combination of lima beans,
   red kidney beans, and cannellini beans),
   or 2 (14-ounce/400 g) cans beans
A pinch of baking soda
1 shallot, halved
1 carrot, halved
1 stalk celery, cut into large chunks
1 garlic clove, halved
1 bay leaf
7 ounces/200 g pork belly, diced
Flaky sea salt and ground white pepper

For the feijoada

2 tablespoons olive oil
2 onions, diced
2 garlic cloves, crushed
2 carrots, diced
1 stalk celery, diced
1 bay leaf
Flaky sea salt and ground white pepper
Smoked paprika
7 ounces/200 g chouriço
   (skin removed), diced
8½ ounces/250 g morcela, cut into
   thick slices
7 ounces/200 g canned chopped tomatoes
   or 6 ripe plum tomatoes, chopped
3½ ounces/100 g Savoy cabbage,
   thinly sliced
Extra-virgin olive oil, to serve
A large handful of parsley leaves,
   finely chopped

A well-made *feijoada*, in my opinion, is a fantastic thing: a bean and cabbage stew with a bit of cured meat dotted around. My version is fresher and more fragrant than the traditional one and, thanks to the types of meat used, the cooking time is reduced. I use dried beans, as the cooking liquor adds extra flavor to the dish, but if you're in a hurry, a can of good-quality beans is not going to spoil anything.

This recipe uses *chouriço* and *morcela* (blood sausage), but if you can't find either of these just use Spanish chorizo and butcher-shop blood sausage. You could also add some streaky bacon. Serve the *feijoada* with a piece of crusty bread and a glass of Portuguese red wine.

To make the beans — Soak the dried beans overnight in plenty of cold water with a pinch of baking soda to help soften them. The next day, drain the beans, and put them in a pan with the shallot, carrot, celery, garlic, bay leaf, and pork belly. Cover with water and cook over medium heat for 45 minutes to 1 hour, or until tender. Remove from the heat and leave to cool in the cooking liquid. Season the cooking liquid while the beans cool (if you season them during cooking, the skins will harden). Drain the beans, reserving the cooking liquid.

To make the feijoada — Heat the oil in a pan over medium heat. Add the onions and cook gently for 5 minutes, then add the garlic, carrots, celery, and bay leaf. Season with salt, pepper, and paprika and cook until all the vegetables are soft. Add the *chouriço*, *morcela*, and pork belly (if you are using canned beans, and therefore have not cooked it with the dried beans), increase the heat, and cook for 5 minutes, until the meat starts to brown and some of the fat melts out, enhancing the flavor.

Add the tomatoes and stir well. When the tomatoes have sizzled and reduced, pour in 2 cups/500 ml of the bean cooking liquor and 2 cups/500 ml of water (if you have used canned beans, use 1 quart/1 L of water). Bring to a boil and skim as necessary, taking care not to remove the delicious fat, then turn down the heat to low. Stir in the beans and gently simmer for 1 to 1½ hours, or until the pork belly is tender all the way through.

Stir in the cabbage and continue to cook for 5 to 6 minutes, or until tender. Taste for seasoning.

Finish with a drizzle of extra-virgin olive oil and some paprika and chopped parsley on top of each serving. If you have excess liquid left after serving, you could use it as the base for a soup.

Peti

SCOS

Little plates of this and that, small dishes for sharing: these are *petiscos*. They're not a meal in themselves, and are more for the peckish than the ravenous. Most often they're eaten in the mid- to late afternoon, usually accompanied by a cold beer or a glass of crisp *vinho verde*, a green-tinged white wine from Minho in the far north.

The word *petiscos* is often translated as "tapas," but although they're akin to their Spanish cousins and the concept of picking at small things is the same, we Portuguese like to think that ours are different and, of course, better (we would, wouldn't we—our far larger neighbor was historically our biggest rival). *Petiscos* are mostly served on *pratinhos*, little plates; sometimes they're eaten with no cutlery, but the more refined dishes require a fork or spoon.

People will happily eat a few *petiscos* on their own, but they're more often a convivial affair, shared with friends or family—the Portuguese love nothing more than eating and drinking together. The tradition of eating *petiscos* began many years ago with the annual pig slaughter, when men would keep the pigs' ears as little tidbits, taking them back to the local tavern and asking for them to be cooked, then sitting down together and wolfing down their spoils. The ritual pig killing only happened once a year, but this jolly affair soon graduated into men gathering together whenever they felt like it, usually in the afternoon. These days, the *petisco* habit is no longer a "man thing," as many older women would once have claimed with a laugh, and in cities like Lisbon the chefs tend to put a spin on the classics according to their own whim and the ingredients available.

A typical selection of *petiscos* might consist of peanuts or olives, lupini beans, ham, and a round of gooey Serra da Estrela cheese. Seafood is always great—sometimes it's just lightly steamed for a few minutes and that's it. I really love *lulas com alho, malagueta e feijão verde* (Garlic and Chile Squid with Green Beans; page 177), and *Pica Pau* (Quick-Fried Beef with Pickles; page 188).

Preparing a simple *petisco* often involves nothing more than the opening of a tin of fish or seafood. At one time, the canning industry in Portugal was huge: all along the coast there were factories specializing in preserving, but a decline in consumption meant that many family businesses had to close. Some small companies have turned the trend around by designing bright, eye-catching tins—particularly for sardines—and using only the very best quality ingredients. At my restaurant, I decided to make my own mackerel "tins." This gives my team maximum control over flavor and texture, and we forgo the final act of sealing the tin. They are served in the midafternoon—*petisco* time—and I have adapted the recipe for you, without the tins, on page 162.

To me, it doesn't get much better than sharing five or six plates of good food with friends, picking at this and that, talking for hours, and then leaving with a satisfied glow. Many of the recipes that follow are for slightly more considered *petiscos* than you might find in your average *tasca*, such as Cod Cured in Red Pepper Paste (page 173), Grilled Mackerel with Melting Tomatoes (page 171), and Mussels with Chouriço, Tomato, and Peppers (page 180). The unifying theme is that they're small plates to be shared; they're not lunch and they're not dinner, but you could break the rules and make them for either.

Peas and fava beans with cornbread crumbs *Salada de favas e ervilhas*

Serves 2

5 to 7 ounces/150 to 200 g podded
    fresh peas (about 10 to 14 ounces/
    300 to 400 g in their pods)
5 to 7 ounces/150 to 200 g podded and
    peeled fresh fava beans (about 2 to
    3¼ pounds/900 g to 1.2 kg in their pods)
2 handfuls cilantro, 1 handful mint
    and 1 handful parsley leaves, finely
    chopped, plus a few whole leaves
    to garnish
2 teaspoons/10 ml Chardonnay vinegar or
    other good-quality white wine vinegar
1 small shallot, finely chopped
3 to 5 tablespoons/50 to 70 ml extra-virgin
    olive oil, plus extra to serve
Smoked paprika
Flaky sea salt and ground white pepper
Freshly squeezed lemon juice
1 slice Cornbread (page 299), sourdough,
    or other rustic loaf
1 egg yolk

This is a lovely *petisco* to serve on a spring afternoon with other small dishes, or perhaps as an accompaniment to a simple grilled meat or fish dish. In peak season I don't bother to remove the peels from fava beans or the pods from peas, because they are perfectly sweet. Chopped cooked egg yolk is a common Portuguese salad garnish, but here the raw yolk is stirred in to add richness, a bit like a steak tartare.

If the peas and beans are sweet and small enough, there's no need to cook them. Cook any larger or older ones in boiling salted water for 1 to 2 minutes, or until just tender. Drain and immediately plunge them into iced water. Remove the peels from the fava beans once cold.

Make the dressing by combining the herbs, vinegar, shallot, and olive oil in a bowl. Season with paprika, salt, pepper, and lemon juice. Pour the dressing over the peas and fava beans and stir well.

Preheat the oven to 430°F/220°C (convection 390°F/200°C). Put the cornbread on a baking sheet and drizzle each side with olive oil. Toast in the oven until golden brown and crispy. Once cooled, roughly chop into coarse breadcrumbs.

Just before serving, stir the egg yolk into the peas and beans. Finish the salad with a sprinkle of breadcrumbs, some cilantro, parsley, and mint leaves, and a drizzle of extra-virgin olive oil.

Black-eyed pea, red pepper, and apple salad *Salada de feijão frade com maçã*

Serves 4

For the peas

6 ounces/180 g dried black-eyed peas

A pinch of baking soda

1 carrot, cut into chunks

1 stalk celery, cut into chunks

1 shallot, halved

1 bay leaf

Flaky sea salt and ground white pepper

For the salad

2 shallots, finely diced

1 large red pepper, seeded and diced

2 Granny Smith apples, peeled and diced

3 tablespoons extra-virgin olive oil

1 tablespoon Chardonnay vinegar or
   other good-quality white wine vinegar

Freshly squeezed juice of 1 lemon

Flaky sea salt and ground white pepper

A small handful of parsley, leaves
   finely chopped

The combination of black-eyed peas with apple and red pepper makes a lovely, light, refreshing salad. Here I am using dried peas for flavor, but you could use canned peas if you prefer. It's important to leave the salad to marinate for an hour before serving to allow the flavors to develop. I love to eat this with fish, but it works equally well as a light lunch by itself or with Grilled Piri Piri Chicken (page 135).

To cook the peas — Soak the peas overnight in plenty of cold water with the baking soda. The next day, drain the peas and put them in a pan with the carrot, celery, shallot, and bay leaf. Cover with cold water, bring to a boil, and simmer over medium heat for 45 minutes to 1 hour, or until tender. Remove from the heat and leave the peas to cool in the cooking liquid, seasoning them with salt and pepper while they cool.

To make the salad — Drain the peas and put them in a large bowl. Mix in the shallots, red pepper, and apple. Add the oil, vinegar, and lemon juice, season with salt and pepper, and stir well. Leave to marinate at room temperature or in the fridge (I like eating it chilled). Just before serving, stir in the chopped parsley and taste for seasoning.

Tomato and strawberry salad
Salada de tomate e morangos

Serves 4

1 shallot, thinly sliced into rings
Flaky sea salt and ground white pepper
2 thin slices sourdough (it helps if
    you freeze the loaf before slicing it)
2 tablespoons olive oil
1⅓ pounds/600 g mixed heirloom tomatoes
7 ounces/200 g strawberries, ideally small
    ones for the best flavor and sweetness
Extra-virgin olive oil
A small handful of parsley leaves,
    finely chopped
Sherry vinegar (optional)

Some Portuguese dishes can be quite heavy, but this salad is lighter; it's something a bit different that, if you think about it, makes logical use of two ingredients that come into season at the same time, and often even grow alongside each other. The acidity and sweetness of tomatoes and strawberries go together surprisingly well. If you think either of them needs a little extra touch of sweetness, cut them in half and sprinkle superfine sugar on the cut side, then leave in a warm place for a couple of hours before making the salad. You could also try combining tomatoes with apricots, plums, or nectarines, when in season. The salad is lovely on its own, and also goes well with grilled fish.

Put the shallot in a bowl with a pinch of salt and add water to cover, to get rid of a little of its punch.

Preheat the oven to 430°F/220°C (convection 390°F/200°C). Put the bread on a baking sheet and drizzle both sides with the olive oil. Toast until golden brown and crispy. Remove and allow to cool, then break into bite-size pieces.

Cut the tomatoes into roughly equal pieces. Remove the green stems from the strawberries and slice them in half lengthwise. Set aside about a quarter of the strawberries, including any broken or bruised ones, and mash them with a fork.

Put the sliced strawberries and tomatoes in a bowl. In another bowl, mix the mashed strawberries with enough extra-virgin olive oil to form a loose dressing, along with a pinch of salt and the parsley. Stir gently and check the seasoning. If you like, you can add a dash of sherry vinegar, keeping in mind how sweet your tomatoes and strawberries taste. Pour it over the fruit. Drain the shallot rings and sprinkle them on top, then finish with the toast pieces. You can leave this salad to marinate for 1 hour, but it is best eaten on the day it is made.

Watercress salad with fennel and orange
Salada de agrião com funcho e laranja

Serves 4

1½ ounces/40 g sliced almonds

3 tablespoons extra-virgin olive oil

Freshly squeezed juice of 1 orange

Freshly squeezed lemon juice

Flaky sea salt and cracked black pepper

Smoked paprika

2 oranges

1 fennel bulb

5 ounces/150 g watercress

The abundant watercress fields of Portugal inspired this salad. When I'm making it, I dress the orange and fennel first, then add the watercress just before serving, as it's a fragile green and will wilt if left out too long. You can adjust the acidity depending on what you serve it with—it's great for cutting through rich meats, and is particularly delicious with a grilled pork steak or slow-roasted pork.

Preheat the oven to 355°F/180°C (convection 320°F/160°C). Put the almonds on a baking sheet and toast until light golden brown, then remove and set aside to cool.

Make the dressing by whisking together the olive oil, orange juice, lemon juice to taste, and half of the almonds. Season with salt, pepper, and paprika. Cut the peel off the oranges and cut each segment out of the membrane. Trim the fennel, halve it lengthwise, and thinly slice it, preferably with a mandoline. (Fennel discolors quickly, so if you need to slice it beforehand, store it in iced water with a squeeze of lemon juice, and drain it well before making the salad.)

Put the orange segments and fennel in a bowl and pour the dressing on top. Taste for seasoning. Gently add the watercress and finish by sprinkling the reserved almonds on top.

Endive, pear, fennel, and almond salad

Salada de endivias com pera, funcho, e amêndoa

Serves 4

2 ounces/60 g sliced almonds

3 firm but ripe pears, such as Comice

2 heads Belgian endive

1 large fennel bulb

For the dressing

1 orange, peeled and quartered

3 heirloom or vine-ripe
    tomatoes, quartered

½ garlic clove, crushed

1 red pepper, seeded and coarsely chopped

1 small slice stale sourdough or other rustic
    loaf, torn into pieces

1 teaspoon smoked paprika

4 tablespoons sherry or red wine vinegar

1 teaspoon honey

Freshly squeezed lemon juice, to taste

6 tablespoons extra-virgin olive oil

A dash of Amaretto (optional)

This salad isn't typically Portuguese, but the dressing takes its inspiration from the smoky flavors of the classic marinade *massa de pimentão* or red pepper paste (page 173). Along with the smokiness, the salad has a lovely combination of crunch, sweetness, and bitter notes from the endive. The Portuguese aren't generally all that fond of bitter flavors, but they are very good for us.

Preheat the oven to 355°F/180°C (convection 320°F/160°C) and toast the almonds on a baking sheet until light golden brown. Remove from the oven and leave to cool.

To make the dressing — Blend all the dressing ingredients, apart from the olive oil and Amaretto, in a food processor. Once smooth, blend in the olive oil to emulsify it. The dressing should be creamy, with a sharp kick. You could add a dash of Amaretto now, if you like, for extra sweetness to contrast with the bitterness of the endive and the anise taste from the fennel.

Halve the pears lengthwise, remove the core, and thinly slice them. Once ready to serve, halve the endive lengthwise and separate out the leaves. Trim and thinly slice the fennel with a knife or mandoline, keeping the lovely green fronds as a garnish. (You could do this a little in advance, in which case put the endive and fennel in iced water to preserve their color and crispness, then drain well before assembling the salad.)

Put the endive, fennel, and pear in a large serving bowl. Pour over the dressing and sprinkle the toasted almonds and fennel fronds on top.

Carrot salad with toasted hazelnuts and honey *Cenouras com mel e avelãs*

Serves 4

1½ ounces/40 g blanched hazelnuts

17 ounces/500 g heirloom carrots, scrubbed and trimmed

Fine sea salt

2 tablespoons extra-virgin olive oil

3 tablespoons/50 ml freshly squeezed orange juice

1½ teaspoons/10 g honey

2 teaspoons/10 ml sherry vinegar

Flaky sea salt and ground white pepper

Smoked paprika

A small bunch of chives, finely chopped

A small bunch of chervil, finely chopped

For the pickle liquid

2½ cups/600 ml Japanese rice vinegar

3 cups/600 g superfine sugar

3 tablespoons/50 g fine sea salt

2 bay leaves

½ teaspoon black peppercorns

You can buy heirloom carrots from farmers' markets and good greengrocers; I like to use a selection of colors—purple, orange, yellow, white—for a rainbow salad. If your carrots have lovely fresh tops, you can use these as a garnish along with the herbs. I prefer to scrub rather than peel them, as it helps keep their natural shape and flavor. It's up to you how you split the combination of fresh, fermented, and pickled carrots, but I prefer to use mostly fresh, with equal quantities of pickled and fermented. The salad works well by itself (I like it with fresh ricotta or burrata), or as a side for the Cod Baked in a Cornbread Crust on page 211. You'll need to allow a few days for pickling and marinating.

Preheat the oven to 355°F/180°C (convection 320°F/160°C). Put the hazelnuts on a baking sheet and toast until light golden brown, then remove and set aside to cool.

Make fermented carrots by cutting some of them into thick batons (the amount is up to you; see the headnote). Weigh these and put them in an airtight container. Add 2 percent of their weight in fine sea salt, mix well, cover, and leave to ferment for 3 to 4 days in a warm place, until they become sour.

Make pickled carrots by slicing some of them into 1-inch/ 2- to 3-cm rounds. Dissolve the pickle liquid ingredients with 2½ cups/600 ml of water in a small pan over low heat. Cool a little, then pour over the carrots. Store in an airtight container for 2 to 3 weeks, depending on how crunchy you like them.

Using a wide vegetable peeler, peel thin, wide strips of the remaining (raw) carrots. You could also slice them as thinly as you can with a sharp knife.

Whisk together the olive oil, orange juice, honey, and sherry vinegar and season with salt, pepper, and paprika. You could also add a splash of the juice from the fermented carrots or some of the pickle liquid, if you like. Mix together the fresh, fermented, and pickled carrots. Pour the dressing over the carrots and leave to marinate for a couple of hours. Just before serving, sprinkle the herbs over the carrots and stir well.

Garlic and turnip green rice with piri piri oil *Arroz de grelos*

Serves 4

For the piri piri oil

5 to 7 fresh piri piri, malagueta, or
    bird's eye chiles
4 garlic cloves, finely chopped
1 teaspoon fine sea salt
1¼ cups/300 ml olive oil
10 dried piri piri or malagueta chiles
2 tablespoons brandy or aguardente velha
Finely grated zest of 1 lemon
1 tablespoon lemon juice
1 tablespoon white wine vinegar
3 bay leaves
A few black peppercorns

For the rice

4 tablespoons olive oil
1 white onion, finely diced
2 garlic cloves, crushed
A small bunch of turnip greens, leaves and
    stems finely chopped
1½ tablespoons/20 g butter
1 cup/200 g short-grain white rice,
    preferably Portuguese Carolino,
    Japanese sushi, or Spanish Bomba rice
1 quart/1 L vegetable stock or water
3½ ounces/100 g lacinato kale, stalks
    removed and coarsely chopped
A small bunch of cilantro leaves,
    finely chopped
Freshly squeezed lemon juice
Extra-virgin olive oil, to serve
Flaky sea salt and ground white pepper

Portuguese *arroz* (rice) dishes change with the seasons, with variations that feature ingredients such as tomato, clams and cilantro, *farinheira* (smoked sausage), or kidney beans. *Grelos* (large turnip greens) are almost sacred—we can't get enough of them. Fried with garlic, turnip greens make for an *arroz* that's perfect on its own or alongside a lovely piece of grilled meat or fish. There's a ritual to finishing a Portuguese rice dish: you adjust the seasoning at the end, add herbs, citrus, and plenty of Portuguese olive oil, and stir vigorously before serving.

I like mine with a bit of piri piri oil, the ubiquitous spicy oil that we drizzle on soups, *açordas*, roasted vegetables, seared meats, softly scrambled eggs, or crusty bread. Stored in a glass jar or bottle at room temperature, it lasts for months, although I seem to use it up quite quickly—I like to add it to just about everything.

To make the piri piri oil — Make a paste with the fresh chiles, garlic, and sea salt using a mortar and pestle or a food processor. Heat the paste with ¼ cup/60 ml of the oil in a small pan over low heat. Add the remaining ingredients, except the remaining oil. Increase the heat to medium and cook for 3 to 4 minutes, to burn off the alcohol and lightly caramelize the garlic and chiles. Remove the pan from the heat and stir in the remaining 1 cup/240 ml oil.

To make the rice — Heat the olive oil in a pan over medium heat. Add the onion, garlic, and turnip greens and cook for about 10 minutes, or until soft. Add the butter and rice to the same pan and cook for a few minutes to toast it. Add the stock and cook over low heat for 10 minutes. Stir in the kale. Cook, stirring occasionally, for about 25 minutes, or until the rice is a little al dente but still has a thick broth-like consistency. Remove from the heat, cover, and let sit for 5 minutes, to enhance the flavors. Stir in the cilantro.

To serve, add a generous squeeze of lemon juice and a glug of extra-virgin olive oil, and, of course, the piri piri oil. Taste for seasoning. Transfer to a warmed serving dish and serve.

Marinated mushrooms with bacon

Cogumelos marinados com bacon

Serves 4

8 ounces/250 g cremini mushrooms

8 ounces/250 g button mushrooms

6 tablespoons olive oil

1 small white onion, thinly sliced

4 thin slices smoky bacon

Flaky sea salt and ground white pepper

1 long red chile, halved lengthwise

5 tablespoons Chardonnay vinegar or
    other good-quality white wine vinegar

5 tablespoons sherry vinegar

Extra-virgin olive oil, to drizzle

A handful of parsley leaves, finely chopped

This is a simple, flavorful snack that you find in many *tascas*, often served with toothpicks. It's a tasty way to use cultivated mushrooms. I was once in Lisbon with someone who was vegan and this seemed like a good dish for her to try. When we ordered it, we were assured that it was vegan. When the dish arrived and we queried what the little pieces of bacon were, the waiter looked at us, astonished, and declared: "That's not meat, it's bacon!" Unfortunately, this is not uncommon in Lisbon, although things are finally changing.

Rinse the mushrooms under running water and drain them (they don't have to be perfectly dry, as a little excess water will help steam them).

Heat the olive oil in a pan over medium heat. Add the onion and bacon and cook for a few minutes, seasoning well with salt and pepper. Add the mushrooms, chile, and vinegars and stir well. Cover and simmer gently for 25 minutes. Remove the pan from the heat and stir in a generous glug of extra-virgin olive oil.

Once cool, mix in the parsley leaves and leave to marinate for a few hours at room temperature before eating. Drain off some of the liquid, if you like (the mushrooms can release quite a lot of liquid), and taste to check the seasoning. I like to serve it piled high on crusty bread, and it would also be great with Marinated Pot-Roasted Chicken (page 219) or Kale Migas with Mushrooms (page 233).

Cured mackerel with tomatoes and fennel *Cavala marinada com tomate e funcho*

Serves 2

For the cured mackerel

7 tablespoons/90 g superfine sugar

3½ tablespoons/60 g fine sea salt

2 strips lemon zest

2 bay leaves

A small handful of parsley, leaves
     picked and stalks separated

2 mackerel fillets, pinboned
     and skin removed

For the tomatoes and fennel

7 ounces/200 g ripe cherry tomatoes

Flaky sea salt and ground white pepper

1 small fennel bulb

A few sprigs of marjoram

2 tablespoons extra-virgin olive oil,
     plus extra for serving

Chardonnay vinegar or other good-quality
     white wine vinegar

For many years there was a tendency to overcook fish in Portugal, but more recently we have started to appreciate the incredible flavor of raw mackerel. The sweetness and fattiness of the fish from cold Portuguese waters is very similar to the mackerel available in the UK, so this recipe translates well when I make it in London. Good-quality fish such as this doesn't need much else—it's a case of following the seasons and pairing it with ingredients that will naturally offset its richness. Early summer tomatoes, still not totally sweet, work perfectly, and at peak season, berries or stone fruits would be excellent too. It's simple but beautiful.

To cure the mackerel — Whisk together the sugar and salt in a bowl until well combined, then spread half the mixture over the bottom of a small shallow baking dish. Add half the lemon zest, bay leaves, and parsley stalks. Put the fish on top and cover with the rest of the flavorings and sugar-salt mixture. Leave to sit at room temperature for 30 minutes, then rinse off the cure and pat dry with paper towels. Dice the mackerel into bite-size pieces.

To prepare the tomatoes and fennel — Slice the tomatoes in half horizontally through the equator. Put them in a bowl and season generously with salt and pepper. Using a mandoline or a sharp knife, shave the fennel very thinly. Add the fennel and marjoram to the tomatoes. Stir in the olive oil and vinegar, to taste, and leave to marinate for 2 hours at room temperature.

Arrange the mackerel on a serving plate with the fennel and tomatoes. I love this with a slice of crusty bread and a generous glug of olive oil.

Marinated tuna with sweet onions
Atum com cebolada

Serves 2

7 ounces/200 g tuna steak, ideally
    sushi grade
Flaky sea salt and ground white pepper
2 tablespoons extra-virgin olive oil
2 tablespoons olive oil
1 red onion, thinly sliced into rings
1 white onion, thinly sliced into rings
1 shallot, thinly sliced into rings
1 garlic clove, crushed
1 bay leaf
2 strips orange zest
1 small cinnamon stick, broken in half
Chardonnay vinegar or other good-quality
    white wine vinegar

This dish is a celebration of the amazing tuna that are plentiful in the pure waters around the Portuguese islands of Madeira and the Azores. The recipe relies on *cebolada*, a method of cooking onions at high heat without browning them, before adding vinegar and aromatics to make a marinade. This should be served at sunset somewhere sunny and warm, ideally with a glass of *vinho verde*, a light-bodied wine from the far north of Portugal.

Season the tuna with salt and pepper and drizzle it with the extra-virgin olive oil, then chill for 2 to 3 hours. As tuna is very delicate and oxidizes quickly, I prefer to keep it in one piece.

Heat the olive oil in a frying pan over medium heat. Add the onions and shallot and cook for 5 minutes, or until lightly caramelized but still slightly crunchy. Season with salt and pepper during cooking. Add the garlic with the bay leaf, orange zest, and cinnamon stick and cook for 2 minutes, or until fragrant. Add a splash of vinegar and cook for another few minutes, then remove from the pan and set aside to cool. You could even make this the day before to let the flavors develop more.

Thinly slice the tuna and stir it into the onions. I like to leave it to marinate for 1 hour before serving at room temperature.

Octopus and tomato salad
Salada de polvo com tomate

Serves 4

For the octopus

1 octopus (about 1⅓ pounds/600 g),
    cleaned, with head, eyes, and
    innards removed

1 small white onion, quartered

2 bay leaves

1 garlic clove

Flaky sea salt and ground white pepper

7 tablespoons/100 ml extra-virgin olive oil

Smoked paprika

For the salad

2 small shallots, thinly sliced into rings

Flaky sea salt and ground white pepper

7 ounces/200 g ripe heirloom tomatoes

Extra-virgin olive oil

Freshly squeezed juice of 1 lemon

A small handful of parsley leaves,
    finely chopped

I eat this salad in the late summer, when the tomatoes are at their finest. There are very few ingredients, so they have to be good quality: use an excellent extra-virgin olive oil and the best-quality octopus you can find. It should have been frozen to tenderize it; check with your fishmonger. In Portugal, octopus is often roasted, but in this recipe it is simmered until tender to make a very refreshing salad.

To cook the octopus — Rinse the octopus under cold running water. Half-fill a large pan with water and add the onion, bay leaves, garlic, and a generous pinch of salt and pepper. Bring the water to a boil. Add the octopus to the pan and boil for 3 minutes, then take it out and leave it to rest for a few minutes. Bring the water to a boil again and repeat the process twice. In this way you can control the cooking process and check how firm the octopus flesh is becoming. At this point, the flesh should be tender but have a little resistance when you insert a knife, and the skin will feel slightly gelatinous.

Turn the heat down to low and simmer the octopus, covered, for 20 minutes. Remove from the pan and leave it to cool. If you have time, chill it overnight, which firms up the flesh. When the octopus has cooled, cut it into equal pieces. Marinate the cooked octopus in a bowl with the olive oil and season with paprika, salt, and pepper.

To make the salad — Put the shallots in a small bowl with enough water to cover them and a pinch of salt, and set aside for a few minutes. Quarter the tomatoes, sprinkle them with salt, and drizzle generously with olive oil. Just before serving, drain the shallots and put them in a bowl with the tomatoes. Add another dash of olive oil, lemon juice to taste, and the parsley and stir well. Arrange the octopus on top and serve right away.

Grilled mackerel with melting tomatoes
Cavala maçaricada em refogado de tomate

Serves 4

For the cured mackerel
A scant cup/180 g superfine sugar
7 tablespoons/120 g fine sea salt
4 strips lemon zest
4 bay leaves
A small bunch of parsley, stalks separated
    and leaves finely chopped
4 mackerel fillets, pinboned, skin on

For the sauce
4 tablespoons olive oil
2 small white onions, thinly sliced
Flaky sea salt and ground white pepper
Smoked paprika
2 garlic cloves, crushed
1 bay leaf
1 long red chile, seeded
    and halved lengthwise
12 ripe plum tomatoes, 8 quartered
    and 4 coarsely grated
Chardonnay vinegar, good-quality
    white wine vinegar, or sherry
    vinegar
Chopped parsley, to serve
Extra-virgin olive oil, to serve

I remember seeing rows of mackerel lined up in some of my favorite *tascas* around Lisbon. You'd go in and order one or two fillets and eat them on a small plate with lots of sauce. They're great enjoyed midafternoon, preferably while sitting outside with a nice cold Portuguese beer or a chilled glass of *vinho verde*. Serve with crusty bread.

To cure the mackerel — In a bowl, mix together the sugar and salt until well combined, then spread half the mixture over the bottom of a small baking sheet. Add half the lemon zest, bay leaves, and parsley stalks. Put the fish on top and cover with the remaining flavorings and the sugar-salt mixture. Leave at room temperature for 30 minutes, then rinse off the cure and pat the mackerel dry with paper towels.

Preheat the broiler to high. Put the mackerel on a baking sheet and broil for 2 to 3 minutes, skin-side up, until the skin colors. Alternatively, use a kitchen blowtorch.

To make the sauce — Heat the olive oil in a pan over low heat. Add the onions and cook gently for 10 minutes, or until soft. Season with salt, pepper, and paprika, then add the garlic, bay leaf, and chile and cook for a few minutes, until fragrant. The trick is to lightly brown the vegetables, rather than sweating them, to get extra flavor; increase the heat if necessary. Add the quartered tomatoes and cook for 10 minutes, or until they are just starting to break down but are not mushy. Remove the pan from the heat, add a splash of vinegar and a little chopped parsley, and check the seasoning. Allow the sauce to cool. Just before serving, add the grated tomatoes.

To serve, spoon a layer of the sauce into a large serving dish and place the cured mackerel on top. Finish with another layer of sauce and a drizzle of extra-virgin olive oil. This is better after it has been left to marinate for a little while, even until the next day; try it for yourself and see.

Cod cured in red pepper paste

Bacalhau com massa de pimentão

Serves 2 to 4

For the red pepper paste

3 red peppers

1 garlic clove

Fine sea salt, for fermenting

3 tablespoons/40 ml Chardonnay vinegar
or other good-quality white wine vinegar
(optional), plus extra to taste

Flaky sea salt and ground white pepper

A generous pinch of smoked paprika
(optional)

For the cured cod

7 ounces/200 g cured cod fillet (page 97)

A few slices of crusty bread

1 garlic clove, halved

Extra-virgin olive oil, for drizzling

Finely grated zest of 1 lemon

I love to eat fish in its raw or cured state; perhaps it's my fascination with Japanese food that brought this about. For this dish, fillets of cod are cured in *massa de pimentão*, a classic Portuguese paste made from fermented red peppers, which is used in sauces, dressings, and marinades. Typically, the peppers are fermented for several days with garlic and salt, and the end product is a brilliant pantry staple, deep red in color and thick in texture. My recipe provides a simpler option for which you don't have to ferment the peppers, and which includes smoky paprika and vinegar to help recreate the fermented flavors. If you can, though, try making the real thing. Store the paste in the fridge, covered with a layer of extra-virgin olive oil. You'll find that the flavor continues to develop.

To make the red pepper paste — Start by fermenting the peppers, if you like. (If using fresh peppers, skip to the next paragraph.) Seed and chop the peppers into equal small pieces. Add the garlic, weigh the mixture, and then add 2 percent of the total weight in fine sea salt. Mix very well and put the mixture on a baking sheet, loosely covered with foil. Heat it in the oven for a couple of hours on the lowest setting possible. Set it aside overnight. The next day, purée it with an immersion blender, then leave to ferment in a sealed plastic container in a warm place for 3 to 4 days. There should be a rich, sour flavor.

If using fresh peppers, preheat the oven to 390°F/200°C (convection 355°F/180°C). Put the peppers on a baking sheet and roast for 20 minutes, or until charred. Put them in a plastic bag, then tie it and leave to cool. Peel the peppers and remove the core and seeds. Using an immersion blender, blend the peppers with the vinegar, garlic, and a generous pinch of flaky sea salt, pepper, and paprika.

The paste can be used as it is or, if you want a thicker one (for marinating meats, for example), you could simmer it gently in a pan, stirring, to reduce the liquid. If you want to make a dressing with it, slowly pour in extra-virgin olive oil in a ratio of two parts paste to one part oil, stirring to emulsify it, and add 4 teaspoons/20 ml Chardonnay vinegar to increase the acidity. →

→ *To prepare the cured cod* — Rinse and dry the cod carefully with paper towels. Put it on a clean sheet pan and spread the red pepper paste on both sides of the fish, ensuring it is completely covered. Leave to marinate for 20 minutes, turning it once.

Preheat the oven to 390°F/200°C (convection 355°F/180°C). Rub the bread with the garlic clove and drizzle with extra-virgin olive oil. Toast in the oven for 5 minutes, or until golden brown and crispy.

Flake the cod gently into large chunks, or slice it thinly with a sharp knife, onto a clean plate. Sprinkle the lemon zest on top and drizzle with extra-virgin olive oil. Serve the toast on the side.

Garlic and chile squid with green beans
Lulas com alho, malagueta, e feijão verde

Serves 4

1 white onion, thinly sliced

Flaky sea salt and ground white pepper

3½ ounces/100 g green beans, topped
  and tailed

2 whole squid tubes, cleaned,
  tentacles removed and reserved
  (ask your fishmonger)

Smoked paprika

4 tablespoons olive oil

1 long green chile, seeded
  and thinly sliced

A small handful of cilantro,
  leaves and stalks finely chopped

2 garlic cloves, crushed

3 tablespoons/45 ml dry white wine

Freshly squeezed lemon juice, plus
  lemon wedges to serve

4 teaspoons/20 g butter

2 tablespoons extra-virgin olive oil

Inspired by the garlic prawns that are synonymous with Lisbon, this preparation of squid is just as tasty and quick to prepare. I love chile and have added green beans too, for a little more substance. One of the two keys to success with this recipe is to use very fresh squid; the other is to add the squid to the pan at the very last minute so that it doesn't overcook and become chewy. Serve it right away with lots of crusty bread to dip into the sauce.

Put the onion in a bowl with a pinch of salt and add water to cover, to get rid of a little of its punch. Cook the green beans in a pan of boiling salted water for 1 to 2 minutes, or until just cooked but still crunchy. Drain and put them in a bowl of iced water to stop the cooking. Once completely cool, drain well.

Slice the squid tubes into ⅛-inch/3 to 4 mm rings and the tentacles lengthwise into sections roughly the same size. Season with salt, pepper, and paprika.

Drain the onion and heat the olive oil in a pan over high heat. When the pan is hot, add the chile, cilantro stalks, and garlic. Cook for 2 minutes. Add the white wine, a squeeze of lemon juice, and the green beans and stir well. Immediately add the butter and, as soon as it melts, add the squid and onion. Cook, stirring, for about 1 to 2 minutes, no longer. Stir in the cilantro leaves and remove the pan from the heat. Season with salt, pepper, and more lemon juice to taste if needed, and finish with the extra-virgin olive oil. Bring the pan straight to the table and serve with lemon wedges. If you really love heat, you can serve more sliced chile alongside—I usually do!

Fish

Lisbon is blessed as a city. Not only does it sit right by the River Tejo, but also the Atlantic Ocean, and its bounty is right on our doorstep. This means that spankingly fresh fish can be on the table just a few hours after being caught, sardines and mackerel still vibrantly black, blue, green, yellow, and silver. Portugal is obsessed with fish, and despite being a really small country, we're third in the world—behind only Iceland and Japan—in terms of how much we eat, consuming almost 137 pounds per person every year. A perfect mix of cold water temperature, light, and salinity means that we have a fabulous diversity of seafood in our waters, as well as great plankton and vegetation for them to feast on. This, in turn, makes the fish dense in flavor.

In Lisbon, the types of fish caught on the nearby coast are *sardinhas* (sardines), *cavalas* (mackerel), and *carapau* (horse mackerel). *Carapau* are pretty much unknown or underrated outside Portugal, but the flesh is sweeter and less fatty than ordinary mackerel. Most of our sardines are caught around Peniche, just over 60 miles north of Lisbon, along with lots of other species. This is a little too far from Lisbon for a day trip, but you can see fishing on a slightly smaller scale when you take the train to nearby Cascais early in the morning and greet the fishermen and -women coming in. Excited seagulls signal their arrival, screaming and circling around the boats as they head back to the harbor. The men and women unload their haul onto carts that are wheeled away to the nearby auction house, where they follow an unusual bidding process: the auctioneer starts at an outrageously high price, which then comes down dramatically until someone is willing to pay what he considers is the right sum.

Cascais is most famous for *polvo* (octopus), caught using a special trap called an *alcatruz* that tempts the cephalopod in but makes it very hard for it to get back out again. Once these were molded out of clay, but they are now made from plastic, and so are not very good for the environment. Almost all the boats in Cascais are dedicated to catching octopus. You used to see men beating them on stones to tenderize them, but nowadays the freezer, which does an equally good job of softening the flesh, makes light of such work.

I love the camaraderie of the fishermen and -women, how they sit down together every lunchtime at outdoor tables to eat seafood they brought in that morning. They cook it incredibly simply, grilling or perhaps lightly steaming it, so that the flavor of the sea is the star of the show.

As a child, I spent many summer days on the southern beaches on the far side of the Ponte de 25 Abril—the beautiful bridge that spans the Tejo—where they use an unusual method of fishing called *arte Xávega*. Two small boats will go across the waves and set out nets in a conical shape. In the past, oxen were used to help drag the nets in once they were full, but now tractors, along with a team of men and women, pull them onto the sand. The sight of the fish being hauled in like this is a spectacle that usually draws a crowd. To be honest, seeing the poor things thrashing about in the nets, taking their last breath, is not something I relish. It seems cruel to me because it is not a clean kill, and far too many small fish are caught up in the process. As a chef, I also think this method ends up bruising the flesh, and I can tell if the fish I'm cooking has been caught this way. It makes me sad, but it is an old tradition and I respect that. As much as I would prefer the line-caught method, I know it is not always possible and can be cost-prohibitive. And I admire the fishermen and -women, who are, after all, the ones risking their lives to fulfill our insatiable craving for fish.

At Fonte da Telha, a very long, sandy beach where they use this method, the fishing season runs from March until October or November. The species in a catch will always depend on the time of year, the water temperature, and the condition of the sea. The workers sort through the piles, throwing the fish into different crates according to their species and size. These workers are covered from head to toe in scales, and if you happen to be nearby when they pull the nets in, you will be too. Luis Miguel fishes here with a team of twenty-one people all summer, and in the high heat of the late afternoon they're dressed in rubber waders. "This is a very old-school type of fishing, only done on the Atlantic coast south of Lisbon," he says. "I love it because every day we spend seven or eight hours on the beach. We have to be clever because the fish make every effort to avoid the nets. Some days they succeed."

One of the totemic symbols of Lisbon is the *varina*, a barefoot woman in traditional dress with a big basket—a *canasta*—of fish on her head. Not so long ago, the *varinas* would sell their wares from door to door, so we didn't have to go to the market to buy our fish. We would eat what was in season, knowing that our trusted *varina* was selling the best of the day's catch. Sadly, this tradition has now been lost. Instead, we turn to a reliable fishmonger, and mine is Açucena Veloso, who has worked at the Mercado 31 de Janeiro in the Saldanha neighborhood for fifty-five years. Jewels of the sea shimmer on her vast, amazing stall. Scabbardfish (*peixe espada*) resemble silver belts, and their brothers, black scabbardfish (*peixe espada preto*), are inky and evil-looking with razor-sharp teeth. There's sea bream (*besugos*), hake (*pescadas*), red mullet (*salmonete*), and red scorpionfish (*rascasso*), which seems more like a sculpture in coral than something you'd eat—but we do, boiling it, then shredding and serving the meat with mayonnaise to make it just as sublime as lobster. I'm always

drawn to the tuna because it's a fish I adore, and here it's so dark and meaty it looks like steak. There are octopuses (*polvos*), cuttlefish (*chocos*), clams (*amêijoas*), mussels (*mexilhões*), razor clams (*lingueirões*), and sweet, juicy shrimp (*camarões*), which are some of the best in the world, especially the ones landed in the Algarve.

And then there are *percebes*, or goose barnacles, which look like aliens' fingers, have the texture of an old handbag, and have a kind of hoof on the end. You'll only find them in Portugal and other parts of the southwestern Mediterranean. Don't be scared of them—they have ambrosial treasure within. You eat the inner tube, and to get to it you need to pinch the outside, make a little hole, and pull. I'm not going to lie—they're hard to get to, but once you've mastered the trick it becomes second nature. Their essence is sealed inside them when they're lightly boiled, ready to burst out into your mouth. Watch out for your clothes, though: the juices have a habit of squirting all over you.

Percebes cling to rocks, down which hunters clamber, or onto which they jump from boats. In thrashing Atlantic seas, it can be a very dangerous business, but *percebes* are almost as prized as caviar, and so earn a good price for these brave souls. They're called goose barnacles in English because people in the Middle Ages believed they were embryonic barnacle geese, quietly developing into fledglings on the rocks that would eventually hatch and fly away. This was all in the days before we knew about migration, of course.

Portuguese people are completely infatuated with *bacalhau* (salt cod), which is almost a national symbol. It's called the *fiel amigo* (faithful friend), and the country is so loyal in return that there are said to be more than 365 different ways to cook it. Portugal is a Catholic country, so the tradition of abstaining from meat on Fridays and in the run-up to major feast days means that people often used to turn to *bacalhau*. It's also eaten on Christmas Eve, when *bacalhau de Consoada* comes with potatoes, chickpeas, cabbage, and hard-boiled eggs. (I must say, though, that my own family never stuck to this; we used to eat suckling pig, turkey, or *cabrito*, or young goat, instead.)

The Portuguese love of salted cod goes back many centuries. The Vikings are believed to have been the first people to preserve cod, and they brought the method with them when they came to Portugal in the ninth century, drawn to the country's northern salt plains. In the late fifteenth century, Portuguese fishermen set sail around Newfoundland's Grand Banks to fish for cod, which grew steadily in popularity. During the Discoveries era, when Portuguese ships set sail for every corner of the globe, salt cod was loaded into the hold as a valuable, lightweight, easily stored form of protein that would sustain a crew on their lengthy voyage.

Centuries later, the Portuguese dictatorship known as Estado Novo, which had begun in 1933, started heavily promoting the consumption of cod. The regime launched a "cod campaign," which meant the fishing, salting, transporting, supplying, and pricing of *bacalhau* were

all state controlled. The fall of the regime in 1974 and the depletion of cod around the Grand Banks marked the end of the Portuguese cod industry, and these days we rely on Norway and Iceland for our supply.

Like fado music, salt cod evokes an element of *saudade*, or nostalgia, for a time when Portugal was a strong nation of brave mariners conquering the world. To many of my compatriots, *bacalhau* is the very essence of being Portuguese. But I have a big confession to make here, one that I know is controversial from the mouth of a *lisboeta*: I prefer fresh cod. To me, the taste of *bacalhau* is quite strong—it has an almost fermented flavor, which I do like, but I find the texture too fibrous. I think the beauty of fat flakes of cod is lost, its luminous sweetness gone. I'll no doubt be declared a traitor for voicing this radical opinion, but times have changed—we have refrigeration, ice, and quick transportation; we're not heading out on voyages across two oceans that last years on end; and, unlike in the time of the Discoveries, fresh cod is readily available. I prefer to lightly cure my fish (see page 97).

Of course, I'm not saying that when you go to Portugal you shouldn't try salt cod, or venture into the shops where you'll find it stacked up on marble shelves in piles that grow particularly high in November and December. It is pretty stinky stuff, though, so be prepared for the pungent smell of brine and dried fish wafting out of shop fronts and across the aisles in supermarkets. *Lisboetas'* knowledge of fish is huge. We have always made an effort to know about it because we don't want to be cheated into buying something bad. We insist on eating fish in season; we all know which fish is best at which time of year, and that sardines caught in winter are fit only for canning. Seafood is a part of our DNA, but I didn't fully realize this until I began traveling abroad and discovered that many people elsewhere had never come across whole fish before. In Lisbon, we usually want ours served with their heads, tails, and bones, knowing that cooking fish like this gives it the best flavor.

So, adopt a *lisboeta* state of mind when you buy and eat fish. Do what we do and seek out shiny, shimmering produce that almost looks as if it's still alive. The eyes should be beautiful, really super clear and vibrant. If you touch the fish it should be firm and tense like a hard muscle—rigor mortis is a sign that it is really fresh. It should never smell, and the gills should be pristine, perhaps with just a little bit of muck.

I asked my fishmonger to share some tips to help when shopping for fish. She shrugged, saying, "I only sell fish that I like, that hasn't traveled far at all so it is really fresh. If it's not good, I won't sell it." Her reply made the secret clear: strike up a relationship with a fishmonger who will turn their nose up at anything other than the best.

Mussels with chouriço, tomato, and peppers *Mexilhões com chouriço, tomate, e pimentos*

Serves 2

1 red pepper

2 tablespoons extra-virgin olive oil

1¾ pounds/800 g mussels

3½ ounces/100 g chouriço
   (skin removed), diced

1 small white onion, thinly sliced into rings

7 ripe plum tomatoes, coarsely chopped

2 tablespoons dry white wine

Flaky sea salt and ground white pepper

A small handful of cilantro leaves,
   finely chopped

Mussels are plentiful along the Portuguese coast. In this recipe I use *chouriço*, tomatoes, and smoky, sweet peppers to flavor these beauties—not unlike the way many *cervejarias* (beer houses) and *marisqueiras* (shellfish restaurants) around Lisbon serve them.

Preheat the oven to 465°F/240°C (convection 430°F/220°C). Put the pepper on a baking sheet, drizzle it with 1 tablespoon of the olive oil, and roast until the skin has blackened. Alternatively, cook it on a gas stove, placing it directly over the flame and turning it regularly. Put it in a bowl, cover with plastic wrap, and leave to cool. Once cooled, peel off the skin and slice the flesh into thin strips.

Wash and debeard the mussels under plenty of cold running water. Discard any that have open shells.

Heat the remaining 1 tablespoon olive oil in a pan over medium heat. Add the *chouriço* and cook gently until it starts to crisp around the edges. Add the onion and cook until soft, then stir in the red pepper and tomatoes. Gently tip in the mussels and white wine and stir a few times to evaporate some of the white wine. Cover and steam the mussels for 3 to 4 minutes, shaking the pan while cooking so that all the mussels open (remove and discard any that do not open). Season lightly with salt and pepper.

Stir in the cilantro, transfer to a serving bowl, and serve immediately, spooning the juices over the mussels.

Portuguese dressed crab
Santola recheada

Serves 2

1 crab, such as blue crab or
    Dungeness crab

Your choice of seasonings
Tabasco
Worcestershire sauce
Finely grated zest and juice of 1 lemon
Brandy
Ketchup
Mustard
Gherkins, finely chopped
Pickled vegetables (page 188)

To serve (optional)
Shallots, finely chopped
Parsley, leaves finely chopped
Hard-boiled eggs, yolks and
    whites grated separately

The crabs in Portugal are fabulous. *Santola* (spider crab) and *sapateira* (similiar to the brown crab) are available at most *marisqueiras* (shellfish restaurants), and we serve them a bit like traditional dressed crab: you gently smack the legs and claws with a hammer to extract the sweet meat inside, which you dip in a mix that we call *caça* and eat with a little toasted crusty bread. The *caça* varies, but usually includes pickled vegetables, grated egg, and a shot of brandy. The rest depends on the creativity and patience of the chef.

Bring a large pan of water to a boil, add the crab, and simmer for 12 to 15 minutes (for a 2-pound/1 kg crab), or until it is cooked through. Check by breaking off one of the claws: the meat inside should be white and opaque. Remove the crab and put it in a bowl of ice to cool.

Twist off the claws and set them aside. Put the crab on its back with the eyes facing toward you. Press your thumbs on either side of the eyes and push away the shell. Discard the grayish, feathery-looking gills (called "dead men's fingers"), which are poisonous and should not be eaten.

Use a crab picker or skewer to pick the white meat from the body. Scrape out the brown meat from the shell. In a bowl, mix together the white and brown meat, then add your choice of seasonings. I like to add brandy, a bit of ketchup and mustard, and some finely chopped pickled vegetables.

To serve — Spoon the filling into the main body shell. Crack the backs of the claws and legs with a heavy spoon or knife and arrange them around the shell. Garnish the crab with finely chopped shallots and parsley; grated egg yolk and white is also a wonderful addition.

Scrambled eggs with smoked
sausage *Ovos mexidos com farinheira*

Serves 4

6 eggs

Flaky sea salt and ground white pepper

1 good-quality farinheira sausage
    (about 7 ounces/200 g)

2 tablespoons olive oil

1 zucchini, thinly sliced into rounds

A small handful of parsley leaves,
    finely chopped

Freshly squeezed lemon juice

Scrambled eggs and *farinheira* (smoked sausage) is one of my favorite egg dishes ever. In Portugal we eat it as a *petisco* in the late afternoon, together with several other small plates. It really is worth getting hold of real Portuguese *farinheira*— this may require a little planning, but once you source some (it's available online), I'm sure you will use it a lot. Serve this with plenty of crusty bread.

Whisk the eggs in a bowl and season them with salt and pepper. Take the *farinheira* out of its casing and break it into small pieces. Heat the olive oil in a frying pan over medium heat, add the *farinheira* and cook for a few minutes, until crisp around the edges. Add the zucchini to the pan and cook for 2 minutes, or until lightly cooked.

Pour the eggs into the pan and cook gently, folding them with a wooden spoon, until they are soft and creamy, seasoning them with salt and pepper. Be careful not to overcook the eggs; remove the pan from the heat just before they are fully cooked. Stir in the parsley and add a squeeze of lemon to taste, then serve immediately.

Quick-fried beef with pickles *Pica pau*

Serves 4

For the pickled vegetables
2½ cups/600 ml Japanese rice vinegar
3 cups/600 g superfine sugar
3 tablespoons/50 g fine sea salt
2 bay leaves
½ teaspoon black peppercorns
1 small head cauliflower, cut into
    bite-size florets
2 carrots, cut into ⅓-inch/5 mm slices
1 onion, cut into eighths

For the pica pau
1 tablespoon good-quality rendered pork fat
1 tablespoon olive oil
1 garlic clove, smashed
1 small long red chile, seeded
    (optional) and halved lengthwise
10 ounces/300 g beef filet, rump, or sirloin,
    cut into bite-size pieces
Flaky sea salt and ground white pepper
5 ounces/150 g thick-cut cured ham,
    ideally Ibérico, Serrano, or
    Parma ham, finely chopped
10 small gherkins, finely chopped
About 1 tablespoon dry white wine
A small handful of parsley leaves,
    finely chopped
Lemon wedges, to serve
Piri piri oil (page 156), to serve

Pica pau means "woodpecker," and you eat this dish with a toothpick, picking pieces up and gobbling them a bit like its namesake. My version uses beef filet; if you ask your butcher to give you the tail ends of the filet it will be a lot cheaper, without compromising on flavor. I use Ibérico ham for its rich, sweet flavor. You could use other cured hams, but remember to check the salt content, because some types are saltier and less nutty than Ibérico. When I dream of this dish, which I often do, it always comes with a nice ice-cold draft beer.

To make the pickled vegetables — Put the rice vinegar, sugar, salt, bay leaves, and peppercorns in a pan with 2½ cups/ 600 ml of water. Place over medium heat and cook until the sugar has dissolved. Increase the heat and bring it to a boil, then add the cauliflower, carrots, and onion. Remove from the heat and transfer to a bowl to cool, along with the liquor. I like to make this the day before I use it. Stored in an airtight container, it should keep for 2 weeks in the fridge.

To make the pica pau — Take a handful of the pickles and cut them into small pieces, then set aside. Melt the pork fat and olive oil over high heat in a large frying pan. When the fat starts to sizzle, add the garlic, chile, and beef and season with salt and pepper. Sauté quickly for 2 to 3 minutes.

Stir in the ham, chopped pickled vegetables, and gherkins, then add the white wine, starting with ½ tablespoon and adding more to taste as required, along with a splash of pickling liquid if you like. Sauté for another minute. Take the pan off the heat and stir in the parsley. Serve immediately, in the pan, with toothpicks. Lemon wedges and a drizzle of piri piri oil are nice additions.

Crispy pig's ear salad

Salada de orelha de porco

Serves 4

Fine sea salt, to cover
3 pigs' ears, cleaned
1 shallot, halved
1 bay leaf
A few black peppercorns
2 tablespoons olive oil
2 oranges (preferably blood oranges)
    or 1 large grapefruit
1 small white onion, finely diced
4 tablespoons extra-virgin olive oil
1 tablespoon sherry vinegar
A small handful of cilantro
    leaves, roughly torn
Flaky sea salt and ground white pepper
Smoked paprika

It is a domestic tradition in Portugal to slaughter a pig every year in a ritual called the *matança*. At our family farm in the Alentejo region, we used do it in January when the pigs were extra fat because of the cold. Every part of the animal was used: the legs for hams; the blood in a flavored rice; the intestines as casings for *chouriço* or *morcela*; the fat rendered down to make lard; and the ears salted for a couple of hours, then fried and added to a lovely salad. Here is our family recipe for that dish, in which the acidic notes of the orange and sherry vinegar are perfect with the crispy ears. You'll need to start preparing the pigs' ears the day before you want to eat them.

Sprinkle a light layer of sea salt over the pigs' ears and chill for 2 hours in the fridge. Rinse off the salt and pat dry with paper towels. Put the ears in a pan with water to cover and the shallot, bay leaf, and black peppercorns. Simmer gently for 2 hours, or until cooked through.

Put the ears on a baking sheet, cover with baking parchment, and put a weight on top to press them down (I normally use a can of beans). Chill overnight, ideally for 24 hours.

Heat the olive oil in a large frying pan over high heat, add the ears, and cook for 4 minutes or so on each side, or until crispy. To make sure they crisp up, press them down but do not move them as they cook. Remove and, once cool enough to touch, dice roughly.

Cut the peel off the oranges and cut out the segments, leaving the membrane behind. Squeeze the juice from the trimmings into a bowl, and add the segments. Add the onion, extra-virgin olive oil, and sherry vinegar. Stir in the pigs' ears and cilantro and season with salt, pepper, and paprika. You can eat it warm or leave it to marinate for a few hours.

Smoked garlic and chicken sausage
Alheira

Makes about 20 sausages

1¾ pounds/800 g (6 to 8) chicken thighs,
   skin on and bone in

1 pound/440 g (about 2) duck legs, skin on
   and bone in

8 bay leaves

1 pound/450 g sourdough or other rustic
   loaf, torn into small pieces

1 teaspoon white pepper, plus extra
   for seasoning

5 garlic cloves, crushed

5 tablespoons smoked paprika

⅔ cup/150 ml white wine vinegar

2 teaspoons flaky sea salt, plus extra
   for seasoning

5 tablespoons/70 ml olive oil

Alheira **was created by the Jewish community in the fifteenth century, when they were forced to convert to Christianity. In a clever bid to assimilate while still observing their religious tradition that forbade the eating of pork, they made their sausages with game meats and hung them in the fireplace to dry, smoke, and ferment gradually, in the same way as the usual pork version. Today,** *alheira* **is revered and eaten by everyone. You'll need sausage casings, butcher's twine, wood chips, and a sausage-making machine or a stand mixer with a sausage attachment for this recipe.**

Put the chicken thighs, duck legs, and bay leaves in a large pan over medium heat, and cover with water. Season with salt and pepper, cover, and simmer over low heat for about 1 hour, or until the meat is cooked through and falls off the bone. Remove the meat from the pan and cool. Flake the meat off the bones and finely chop the meat and skin. Reserve the cooking liquid.

Put the bread in a large bowl and pour over ⅞ cup/200 ml of boiling water. Stir in the meat and the pepper, garlic, paprika, vinegar, salt, and oil. Taste and adjust the seasoning as necessary.

Attach one end of the sausage casing to the feeder tube of the sausage-making machine and push the casing all the way onto the tube. Push the sausage mixture through the top tray with the mixer at low speed. Keep feeding and filling, taking care not to fill it too tightly, then tie a knot to seal each end of the casing using butcher's twine. Tie the sausage into about 6-inch/15-cm lengths. Store them in the fridge for 3 to 4 days, or longer if you like, before smoking them.

Put 8 ounces/250 g wood chips in a large heavy-bottomed roasting pan and set a wire rack inside it. Put the sausages on the wire rack and cover the whole pan with foil. Gently heat the pan until you see a little smoke, then turn the heat off and leave it to sit, covered, for 1 hour. Remove the sausages and chill for a day before cooking them, to allow the meat to rest. Traditionally, we deep-fry them, but they can also be baked in the oven or shallow-fried. We eat them just as they are, or with fried eggs and garlicky turnip greens.

Jan

tar

Dinner is a late affair in Portugal. Like our Iberian neighbors, we don't usually sit down to eat our evening meal until at least 8 o'clock. We love to make this a social event, whether it's around a table in the heart of the home or out in a restaurant with friends. Being together is a huge part of how we think about food—our love of the stuff goes hand in hand with the pleasure we get from sharing it.

Talking the day over, from the mundane mechanics of it all to the beautiful or the political, is a fundamental part of dinner for us. We make proper time for it, and sometimes the hours can languidly roll by until after midnight, if the company is right. These are often quite loud and raucous gatherings, and at a really great dinner you'll come to learn that the Portuguese are not, in any sense, a "quiet" people.

Portugal's difficult economic climate has meant that, over the years, our tables have not always heaved with excess, but even in the most straitened times, our food is invariably delicious. Poverty hit harshly in the regions of Alentejo and Trás-os-Montes, for example, and yet these places gave rise to spectacular dishes that have since been adopted by cooks in Lisbon. The Kale Migas with Mushrooms recipe on page 233 dates back to a time when days-old bread was used to bulk out any animal fats the frugal cook might have collected, and together these basic ingredients became something special.

These days, young people in our capital like to hold dinners at home, taking that old notion of *tertúlia*, or artistic gatherings, out of the cafés and into their own kitchens and dining rooms. Food will always be at the heart of things, but you might also stumble across a writer reading aloud from their latest work or a musician playing their new composition. The Portuguese love having guests in their home, and when you're lucky enough to receive an invitation to an evening like this, you feel blessed.

The recipes here will take a little more time to cook than those in the Lunch chapter but you will, in turn, take more time to enjoy them. Some, like the Slow-Baked Lamb Chanfana (page 215), you can marinate one night, slow cook the following night, and then gradually reheat on the evening of your dinner party while you rustle up some side dishes.

The vegetable dishes you'll find in this chapter are not meant to be sides; recipes like the Vinha d'Alhos–Style Vegetables (page 228) are meals in their own right. Greens and vegetables grow very well in Portugal, but until the recent culinary revolution they were always an afterthought in most chefs' minds. In many traditional kitchens they still are, often served soggy and always as a side to a big fat plate of meat or fish. Therefore, my vegetable recipes are not Portuguese classics per se; they're simply made from wonderful fresh ingredients with the vegetarian in mind, and with a Portuguese influence. Of course, everyone else is welcome to tuck in—and if you do choose to serve them as side dishes despite all I've said, fair enough.

Bringing a few of these dishes together will make for a wonderful Portuguese dinner party; add some glorious red wine from the Douro or Alentejo and lots of laughter and chatter, and you'll have a remarkable night.

Shrimp and shellfish rice 199
Arroz de marisco

·

Confit cod with eggs and crispy potatoes 200
Bacalhau à Brás

·

Red mullet with Spanish sauce 202
Salmonetes com molho à espanhola

·

Portuguese fish stew 205
Caldeirada

·

Clams with chouriço, garlic, and cilantro 208
Amêijoas à Bulhão Pato com chouriço

·

Cod baked in a cornbread crust 211
Bacalhau com broa

·

Alentejo-style pork and clams 212
Carne de porco à alentejana

·

Marinated pork with red pepper paste 214
Lombo de porco assado com massa de pimentão

·

Slow-baked lamb chanfana 215
Chanfana

·

Glazed duck rice with chouriço and lardo 217
Arroz de pato

Shrimp and shellfish rice
Arroz de marisco

Serves 4

5 tablespoons olive oil

2 shallots, diced

1 small onion, diced

1 small fennel bulb, trimmed and
    finely chopped

Flaky sea salt and ground white pepper

Smoked paprika

A bunch of cilantro, leaves and
    stalks finely chopped

2 garlic cloves, crushed

Finely grated zest of 1 lemon

½ long red chile, finely chopped

4 ripe plum tomatoes, coarsely grated

1 cup/200 g short-grain white rice,
    preferably Portuguese Carolino,
    Japanese sushi, or Spanish Bomba rice,
    rinsed according to the package
    instructions

2½ cups/600 ml fish stock or water

3 tablespoons/40 ml white wine

20 mussels, cleaned and debearded

20 clams, purged and scrubbed

16 jumbo shrimp, shelled and deveined

A squeeze of lemon juice

Extra-virgin olive oil, to serve

Piri piri oil (page 156), to serve

In the greatest versions of *arroz de marisco*, rice is cooked in a stock made from the shells and trimmings of as many as ten different types of shellfish, and then the tender morsels of seafood are added at the end. Typically, tomatoes, onions, and cilantro are the other elements that make up this fantastic recipe, and the flavors come together perfectly. It's a great dish to put in the middle of the table and let everyone dig in. If you'd like it less spicy, seed the chile.

Heat the olive oil in a pan over medium heat. Add the shallots, onion, and fennel and cook gently for 10 minutes, or until soft. Season with salt, pepper, and paprika. Add the cilantro stalks, garlic, lemon zest, and chile and cook for a few minutes, or until fragrant. Stir in the tomatoes. Increase the heat to caramelize the tomatoes a little for extra flavor. Add the rice and cook for a few minutes to toast it. Add the fish stock and bring to a boil. Reduce the heat and simmer gently until almost cooked, 15 to 20 minutes.

A few minutes before the rice is ready, add the white wine and tip in the mussels and clams. Cover with a lid and shake a few times. Cook for 3 to 4 minutes, then remove the pan from the heat. Discard any unopened shells.

Taste the rice for seasoning, keeping in mind that the mussels and clams will add extra salt. Add the shrimp to the rice and cook for a few minutes until they turn pink. Stir in a squeeze of lemon juice, a little extra-virgin olive oil, and the cilantro leaves. Serve in shallow bowls, and don't forget the piri piri oil!

Confit cod with eggs and crispy potatoes *Bacalhau à Brás*

Serves 2

For the confit cod
1⅔ cups/400 ml extra-virgin olive oil
1 bay leaf
1 garlic clove, crushed
1 small long red chile, cut into chunks
2 (5-ounce/150 g) cured cod fillets
    (page 97)

For the bacalhau à Brás
Vegetable oil, for frying
7 ounces/200 g potatoes, thinly sliced
    into matchsticks
1 onion, thinly sliced
2 garlic cloves, crushed
5 eggs, lightly beaten
Flaky sea salt and ground white pepper
A small handful of parsley leaves,
    finely chopped
Pitted black olives, thinly sliced

À Brás is a classic cooking style that's synonymous with eggs and crispy potatoes, and it's traditionally prepared with cod. This is a simple recipe using straightforward ingredients, but it's truly special when made the right way. The cod should be cured and gently cooked into a confit, the onions slowly caramelized, and the shoestring fries thin and crisp. In many recipes the eggs are cooked to a hard scramble, but I prefer to add them at the end of cooking so that they gently bind all the ingredients in a creamy mixture. Try it like this if you love soft scrambled eggs. The *à Brás* cooking style can be applied to other ingredients too—shrimp and zucchini, say.

To confit the cod — Put all the ingredients except the cod in a small, deep, heavy-bottomed pan and heat gently to 185°F/85°C, or when the oil just starts to bubble. Remove the pan from the heat and leave it to cool for a few minutes. Carefully slide in the fish and leave it submerged in the oil for 15 minutes, or until it flakes apart nicely. Remove the fish, transfer it to a plate, then gently break it apart into bite-size chunks. Reserve the oil.

To make the bacalhau à Brás — Fill a large, heavy-bottomed pan one-third full with vegetable oil and heat it to 355°F/180°C, or until a cube of bread sizzles and turns golden brown almost immediately. Add the potato matchsticks in batches and cook for a few minutes until golden brown and crispy. Remove with a slotted spoon and drain on paper towels.

Heat 2 tablespoons of the reserved confit oil in a pan over medium heat, add the onion, and cook gently until soft. Add the garlic and cook for a few minutes, until fragrant. Stir in one-third of the potato matchsticks. Add the cod, then fold in the eggs, stirring them gently until they start to thicken and softly scramble, and seasoning with salt and pepper. Remove the pan from the heat and stir in another third of the potato matchsticks. Transfer the mixture to serving bowls and sprinkle the remaining third of the matchsticks on top along with the parsley and black olives.

Red mullet with Spanish sauce

Salmonetes com molho à espanhola

Serves 2

For the sauce
3 tablespoons olive oil
1 large white onion, thinly sliced
2 garlic cloves, thinly sliced
¼ cup/60 ml sherry vinegar
Freshly squeezed juice of 1 lemon
1 bay leaf
A sprig of parsley
3 or 4 red mullet livers (see headnote)

For the red mullet
4 red mullet fillets, pinboned, skin on
   (substitute sea bass or another mild,
   fatty white-fleshed fish)
Flaky sea salt and ground white pepper
Smoked paprika
2 tablespoons olive oil
Extra-virgin olive oil, to serve

This dish is not complex, but it really shines when you cook it with top-quality red mullet, such as the ones found along the Portuguese coast. (If you can't source red mullet, ask your fishmonger for a good substitute, such as sea bass, grouper, or goatfish—ideally, you will use livers from the same species in the sauce.) Ideally, the fish should be deep red in color and the flesh bluish and incredibly sweet. The sauce is an adaptation of *molho à espanhola* (Spanish sauce), and the rich red mullet has a shellfish-like flavor that goes perfectly with it. Despite the fact that we share a long border with Spain, there are very few examples of the Portuguese or Spanish making positive references to each other in their cooking—or, indeed, in anything else.

To make the sauce — Heat the olive oil in a pan over medium heat. Add all the sauce ingredients except the livers and cook gently for about 10 minutes, or until the onion is soft. In a separate bowl, mix the livers with 3 tablespoons/40 ml of water to make a loose paste. Stir this into the pan and cook for another few minutes. Transfer to a bowl and leave to cool to room temperature. Remove the parsley sprig.

To cook the red mullet — Season the fish with salt, pepper, and paprika. Heat the olive oil in a small pan over high heat. Once hot, add the fish skin-side down and sear for 2 minutes on each side. Pour the sauce over the fish and drizzle with extra-virgin olive oil to serve.

Portuguese fish stew
Caldeirada

Serves 4

A pinch of saffron

1 garlic clove, halved

10 ounces/300 g potatoes, such as
 Yukon gold, very thinly sliced

4 tablespoons/50 g butter, cubed

5 ripe plum tomatoes, sliced horizontally

1 white onion, very thinly sliced

1 bulb fennel, trimmed and very thinly sliced

Flaky sea salt and ground white pepper

Smoked paprika

14 ounces/400 g red mullet or sea bass
 fillets, each fillet sliced into 3 pieces

Extra-virgin olive oil, to drizzle

⅞ cup/200 ml white wine

A handful of parsley leaves,
 finely chopped

Caldeirada is a kind of baked fish stew, in which the various types of fish and vegetables are sliced and layered on top of each other before being doused with white wine and extra-virgin olive oil and baked. You can play around with the layers and change up ingredients, but make sure you slice the vegetables very thinly so that they cook at the same pace as the fish.

Pour 1 tablespoon of boiling water over the saffron in a small bowl. Rub the cut garlic clove all around the inside of a shallow baking dish, ideally one with a lid. Arrange half the potatoes in the bottom of the dish and put half the butter on top. Follow with a layer of half the tomatoes, onion, and fennel, then the rest of the potatoes. Season every layer with salt, pepper, and paprika. Make a layer of fish, then the remaining onion and fennel, and finally the remaining tomatoes. Dot the remaining butter on top and drizzle with olive oil. Mix the saffron with the wine and pour it over the dish. Leave to marinate for 1 hour.

Preheat the oven to 355°F/180°C (convection 320°F/160°C). Cover the dish with a lid or foil and bake for 20 minutes. Remove the lid and bake for another 20 minutes. Sprinkle the chopped parsley on top just before serving.

Clams with chouriço, garlic, and cilantro *Amêijoas à Bulhão Pato com chouriço*

Serves 4

2 tablespoons olive oil

2½ ounces/70 g chouriço (skin removed), diced into small pieces

1 garlic clove, thinly sliced

A small bunch of cilantro, leaves and stalks separated and finely chopped

14 ounces/400 g clams, scrubbed and purged

1 tablespoon butter

Lemon wedges, to serve

Piri piri oil (page 156), to serve

This simple, classic recipe relies on top-quality clams. These are cooked quickly with the cilantro stalks, garlic, and oil, then sprinkled with plenty of cilantro leaves and served with a nice squeeze of lemon. I like to add crispy pieces of *chouriço*, too, and it's great to have some nice crusty bread to soak up the juices.

Heat the olive oil in a large pan over low heat. Add the *chouriço* and cook until crispy. Add the garlic and cook gently for a minute or so, until fragrant. Add the cilantro stalks with the clams and butter. Increase the heat, cover the pan, and cook for 3 to 5 minutes, shaking the pan occasionally, until the clams start to open (if the shells are thin this will happen very quickly). Take care not to overcook the clams.

Discard any clams that haven't opened. Remove the pan from the heat, add the cilantro leaves, stir two or three times, and put the lid back on. Take the pan to the table covered, then take the lid off at the table. Serve with lemon wedges and piri piri oil to taste, if you like. I prefer it quite lemony and spicy.

Cod baked in a cornbread
crust *Bacalhau com broa*

Serves 2

5 ounces/150 g Cornbread (page 299),
    sourdough, or other rustic loaf
3 tablespoons olive oil
¼ cup/60 ml dry white wine
1 garlic clove, crushed
Finely grated zest and juice of
    1 lemon, plus lemon wedges
    to serve (optional)
A small bunch of cilantro, leaves and
    stalks finely chopped
Flaky sea salt, ground white pepper,
    and cracked black pepper
2 (5-ounce/150 g) cured cod fillets
    (page 97)
1 large fennel bulb
A large handful of green leaves, such
    as spinach, arugula, or watercress
    (optional)
Extra-virgin olive oil, for dressing

The first time I ate this dish, it was made by a good friend of mine, Luís Lucas. Like my father, João, Luís has never been a professional cook but he knows more about traditional Portuguese cuisine than most chefs. This dish is dedicated to him and to my father, who inspired me to make cooking my path in life. Thank you, and I hope I do you justice. The recipe works best with *broa* (Portuguese cornbread), but you could also use sourdough.

Preheat the oven to 375°F/190°C (convection 340°F/170°C). Cut the cornbread into small chunks, then crumble them into coarse breadcrumbs with your hands (if using sourdough, this may be easier in a food processor). In a bowl, mix the breadcrumbs with 2 tablespoons of the olive oil, the white wine, garlic, lemon zest, and cilantro, and season with salt and white pepper. The mixture should have the texture of a wet dough.

Place the cod on a baking sheet and completely cover it with the breadcrumb mixture. Bake for 20 minutes, or until the cod is cooked through and the crust is golden brown and crunchy.

Meanwhile, trim the fennel and thinly slice it with a mandoline or sharp knife just before serving. Drizzle it with the remaining 1 tablespoon olive oil and season with lemon juice, salt, and cracked black pepper. Mix the leaves in a bowl and dress with extra-virgin olive oil, lemon juice to taste, and salt and cracked black pepper. Serve the cod with the fennel, green leaves, and lemon wedges on the side.

Alentejo-style pork and clams

Carne de porco à alentejana

Serves 4

10 ounces/300 g pork loin or neck,
    cut into small cubes
2 tablespoons rendered pork fat or lard
2 bay leaves
1 garlic clove, smashed
5 tablespoons/70 ml dry white wine,
    plus extra for cooking the clams
A generous pinch of smoked paprika
10 ounces/300 g clams, purged and
    scrubbed
1 tablespoon olive oil
Freshly squeezed orange juice,
    plus orange wedges to serve
A small handful of cilantro leaves,
    finely chopped
Flaky sea salt and ground white pepper
Extra-virgin olive oil, to serve

We're known in Portugal for our pork and clam dishes, and this is the most famous one. As a chef, I often combine seafood and pork in the same dish, which some people find unusual or even unfathomable. I always smile when I hear this, as it's considered perfectly normal back home. The briny clam juices add a delicious savoriness to the meat. Sautéed potatoes would be great with it.

In a bowl, mix the pork with the pork fat, bay leaves, garlic, white wine, and paprika. Cover and leave to marinate in the fridge for 6 hours, or ideally overnight.

Rinse the clams under running water and discard any open ones. Heat the olive oil in a large pan over medium heat. Add the pork and cook for a few minutes, turning it regularly, to color it evenly all over. When the pork is almost cooked, add the clams along with a splash of white wine and orange juice. Cover and cook for 2 minutes, then discard any unopened clams. Remove the pan from the heat, stir in the cilantro, and toss well. Taste for seasoning and drizzle with extra-virgin oil. Serve straight from the pan with orange wedges alongside.

Marinated pork with red pepper paste

Lombo de porco assado com massa de pimentão

Serves 4 to 6

2½ pounds/1.2 kg pork loin, off the bone

Flaky sea salt and ground white pepper

1 tablespoon rendered pork fat
   or lard, melted

⅞ cup/200 g red pepper paste (page 173)

4 tablespoons olive oil

5 garlic cloves, crushed

1 teaspoon smoked paprika

7 tablespoons/100 ml Madeira

4 bay leaves, roughly torn

4 teaspoons/20 g butter

This recipe is fantastic, thanks to the red pepper paste in the marinade, and rubbing the pork with extra paste means you get a nice crust around the meat. I prefer to use a loin with the fatty bits still attached; the meat should cook very slowly so that the fat melts gently and keeps the pork moist. This is lovely as a Sunday roast with some fried potatoes and a sharp green salad, or perhaps the watercress and orange salad on page 153. It's also great in the *bifana* sandwiches on page 280. You'll need to marinate the pork for one or two days in advance.

Rub the pork with a little salt and pepper and chill it for 2 hours. Put the pork in a roasting pan, then mix together the pork fat, red pepper paste, olive oil, garlic, paprika, and Madeira and pour it over the pork. Leave the pork to marinate in the fridge overnight. (Ideally, I like to marinate it for 2 days, making sure to rotate it a few times.)

Preheat the oven to 390°F/200°C (convection 355°F/180°C). Pour 2 tablespoons of water into the roasting pan, scatter the bay leaves under and on top of the pork, and dot the butter on top. Cover with foil and roast for 30 minutes, then turn the oven temperature down to 340°F/170°C (convection 300°F/150°C) and roast for 2 hours. Remove the foil for the last 20 minutes of cooking time. Remove the pan from the oven and leave to rest for 20 minutes before serving.

Slow-baked lamb chanfana
Chanfana

Serves 6

4½ pounds/2 kg lamb shoulder
Flaky sea salt and ground white pepper
4 teaspoons/20 g butter
2 tablespoons rendered pork fat or lard
4 garlic cloves, peeled and smashed
6 tablespoons olive oil
2 teaspoons smoked paprika
2 bay leaves, roughly torn
About 1½ cups/350 to 400 ml red wine
6 ounces/180 g smoky bacon,
    coarsely chopped
3 white onions, sliced

For *chanfana*, lamb is marinated in a clay vessel with all of the ingredients overnight, and then cooked in a hot oven. Because of the long marinating time and cooking, I like to use lamb shoulder, which will have enough fat on it and, because it's a working muscle, is well suited to this slow cooking. The red wine helps the meat break down, so make sure you don't skimp—always use wine that you would be happy to drink. This recipe is perfectly tasty straight after you cook it, but it gets even better after several days. It's nice served with boiled potatoes.

Season the lamb with salt and pepper and put it in the dish you will bake it in. Melt the butter and pork fat in a small pan over low heat. In a bowl, mix together the fat with the garlic, 4 tablespoons of the olive oil, the paprika, and the bay leaves. Pour the marinade over the lamb and add enough red wine to cover it completely. Marinate in the fridge for at least 8 hours, ideally overnight.

Preheat the oven to 340°F/170°C (convection 300°F/150°C). Heat the remaining 2 tablespoons olive oil in a pan over medium heat, add the bacon, and cook until the fat melts and it is crispy. Put the bacon and onions under the lamb and cover it with foil. Roast for about 3½ hours, then remove the foil and roast for 20 minutes more, or until it is tender and almost falling off the bone. Leave to rest for at least 15 minutes before serving.

Glazed duck rice with chouriço and lardo *Arroz de pato*

Serves 6

For the duck legs

4 duck legs, skin on, bone in
Flaky sea salt and ground white pepper
½ small fennel bulb, trimmed
    and coarsely chopped
1 onion, coarsely chopped
1 shallot, coarsely chopped
1 carrot, coarsely chopped
1 stalk celery, coarsely chopped
1 bay leaf
5 parsley sprigs

For the rice

4 tablespoons olive oil
½ small fennel bulb, trimmed and diced
    into small pieces
1 onion, diced into small pieces
1 shallot, diced into small pieces
1 carrot, diced into small pieces
1 stalk celery, diced into small pieces
1¾ ounces/50 g chouriço
    (skin removed), diced
1½ cups/300 g short-grain white rice,
    preferably Portuguese Carolino,
    Japanese sushi, or Spanish Bomba rice
⅓ cup/80 ml port, plus a little extra
    if you like
4 teaspoons/20 ml brandy, plus a little
    extra if you like
Flaky sea salt and ground white pepper
2 strips of orange zest

To finish

1 tablespoon olive oil
2 egg yolks, beaten with a splash of water
10 thin slices chouriço, skin removed
6 thin slices lardo

I'll never forget the first time I broke through the egg glaze of a dish of duck rice with my fork. Traditionally, it's baked in a shallow terracotta dish and the rice hides the duck legs beneath it. I have finished my version with *chouriço* and *lardo*, but you could also use duck fat, duck hearts, or foie gras. Serve it with a green salad, simply dressed with olive oil, lemon juice, and black pepper (arugula and watercress would be nice, for a peppery contrast to the richness). If you fancy a sweet but acidic note, serve the duck rice with segments of orange or clementine—this is how we like to eat it in Portugal.

To cook the duck legs — Heat a large pan over medium-high heat. Season the duck legs lightly with salt and pepper on the skin side and put them in the pan, skin-side down. Cook until the fat has melted and the skin is golden brown and crispy, then remove from the pan.

Put the duck legs in a large pan with the fennel, onion, shallot, carrot, celery, bay leaf, and parsley. Pour in cold water to cover (about 4 cups/1 L, plus extra if needed) and season with salt and pepper. Bring to a boil over medium heat and, just when it starts to boil, turn the heat down to low. Cover and simmer gently for about 1 hour, or until the meat comes away easily from the skin. Skim lightly to remove any scum and some of the fat, but don't remove all the fat, as it's important for the flavor.

Remove the duck legs and set them aside to cool. Strain and reserve the cooking liquor, discarding the vegetables and aromatics. Once cooled, remove the duck meat from the bones and finely chop it along with the skin, then set aside.

To cook the rice — Heat the olive oil in a large pan over medium heat, add the fennel, onion, shallot, carrot, and celery, and cook until caramelized. Add the diced *chouriço* and gently cook until the fat starts to melt and the sausage turns golden brown. Add the rice and cook for 2 minutes, or until lightly toasted, stirring so that the grains are coated with fat and flavor. Pour in the port and brandy and cook for 1 to 2 minutes over high heat →

→ to burn off the alcohol. Turn the heat down to medium and add enough reserved duck cooking liquid to cover the rice, adding water if you need to. Season with salt and pepper and add the orange zest.

Cook over low heat for 40 minutes, stirring only occasionally, until the rice is soft but not fully broken down. You do not want the rice to be mushy, or the texture of the dish will be too soft. (Don't stir it too much, as this will draw out the starch, which can make it gloopy.) When the rice is cooked, taste for seasoning and add a splash more brandy and port if you fancy it. Bear in mind that you will put *chouriço* and *lardo* on top, both of which are salty.

Preheat the oven to 390°F/200°C (convection 355°F/180°C) while the rice is cooking. Remove the rice pan from the heat and stir in the chopped duck meat and skin.

To finish the dish — Lightly grease the bottom of a large baking dish—in Portugal we use a deep terracotta one—with olive oil and pour the rice in. Brush the surface lightly with the beaten egg yolks and arrange the *chouriço* and *lardo* slices across the top. Bake for 5 minutes, or until it is golden brown and the *chouriço* and *lardo* have crisped up. Serve straight from the baking dish.

Marinated pot-roasted chicken
Frango na púcara

Serves 4

1 (2¾-pound/1.3 kg) free-range chicken
Flaky sea salt and ground white pepper
Smoked paprika
7 tablespoons/100 g butter, melted
4 ripe plum tomatoes, chopped
4 tablespoons olive oil
7 tablespoons/100 ml white wine
7 tablespoons/100 ml port
7 tablespoons/100 ml brandy, plus extra
    to taste
5 garlic cloves, peeled and smashed
1 tablespoon Dijon mustard
4 bay leaves
6½ ounces/180 g smoky bacon,
    coarsely chopped
2 onions, sliced
A small bunch of parsley leaves,
    finely chopped

Frango na púcara **is a tasty oven-roasted, one-pot chicken dish. It comes from the town of Alcobaça, north of Lisbon, and is traditionally cooked in a terracotta jug (a cast-iron or earthenware casserole dish with a heavy lid can be used instead). It is important to use a very good-quality organic, free-range chicken for this, one that has spent its life eating in the field. Ideally, it should have been hung for about a week to give it a gamier chicken flavor; if you can encourage your butcher to track this down, you may find it is a revelation. The chicken is then marinated overnight before roasting. This is lovely with fried potatoes.**

Joint the chicken into 8 pieces, or ask your butcher to do it for you. Season the chicken with salt, pepper, and paprika. Combine the rest of the ingredients together to make a marinade and pour this over the chicken in the dish you will roast it in. Leave to marinate for 6 hours, or ideally overnight, in the fridge.

Preheat the oven to 390°F/200°C (convection 355°F/180°C). Roast the chicken for 20 minutes, then turn the oven down to 355°F/180°C (convection 320°F/160°C). Continue cooking for another 40 minutes, or until the juices run clear. Add an extra splash of brandy at the end of cooking, if you like.

Remove the chicken from the oven and leave it to rest for 10 minutes before serving. Serve straight from the dish at the table.

Beef skewers with chouriço and bay leaves *Espetadas de carne com chouriço e louro*

Serves 2

2 tablespoons/30 g butter, plus extra
    for basting
2 garlic cloves, finely crushed
1 bay leaf
2 tablespoons Madeira
8 ounces/250 g beef filet or sirloin,
    cut into medium chunks
Flaky sea salt and ground white pepper
1 small white onion
2½ ounces/70 g chouriço (skin removed),
    cut into ¾-inch/2-cm slices
A small handful of parsley leaves,
    finely chopped
Freshly squeezed juice of 1 small lemon
Piri piri oil (page 156), to serve (optional)

I have a long-abiding memory of eating kebabs of *chouriço* and beef threaded together on twigs from a bay tree and cooked over a wood fire. They were truly incredible: the scent of the bay leaves added an amazing aroma to the meat, and the smoky *chouriço* created the perfect balance of flavor and crunch. If you like, try replacing the beef with thick rings of very fresh squid—*mar e terra* (surf and turf) is one of the best kebab combinations you can get. It's really good served with Fried Cornmeal with Parsley (page 68) and a simple watercress salad with lots of cracked black pepper.

Soak some wooden skewers, or twigs from a bay tree if you have them, in water overnight. This will prevent them from burning. Melt the butter in a frying pan over low heat, add the garlic, bay leaf, and Madeira, and cook until the garlic is fragrant. Remove from the heat and cool to room temperature, then pour it over the beef. Season with salt and pepper. Leave to marinate in the fridge for at least 6 hours, ideally overnight.

Cut the onion in half and separate each half into individual petals. Put them in a bowl, cover with warm water and a pinch of salt, and leave to soak for 10 to 15 minutes. This will make the onion a little less sharp.

Dry the skewers with paper towels. Assemble each one, starting with an onion petal, then a slice of *chouriço*, then a piece of beef. Repeat until the skewer is full, leaving some space at the end so that you can pick it up.

Heat a large frying pan over high heat and brush the pan with butter. When the pan is hot, add the skewers and cook for 2 to 3 minutes on each side, for medium-rare. Baste them regularly with butter during cooking. Remove and leave them to rest. (If using a barbecue, sear the skewers on the hottest spot on the grill for about 3 minutes, then transfer to a cooler spot and cook for 2 minutes more. Keep basting them with the melted butter as they cook.) Heat the cooking juices in the pan, then take it off the heat and stir in the parsley and lemon juice. Pour this sauce over the skewers before serving. I love to add a drizzle of piri piri oil.

Squab escabeche
Escabeche de pombo

Serves 4

2 whole squab, wishbone removed
    (ask your butcher)

For the marinade
4 tablespoons olive oil
2 garlic cloves, crushed
3 tablespoons/40 ml dry white wine
1 cinnamon stick
2 bay leaves
Smoked paprika
Flaky sea salt, ground white pepper,
    and cracked black pepper

For the sauce
7 tablespoons/100 ml olive oil
1 small white onion, thinly sliced
3 garlic cloves, crushed
2 bay leaves
1 cinnamon stick
Flaky sea salt and ground white pepper
2 carrots, scrubbed and sliced
    into ¾-inch/2-cm rounds
1 red pepper, seeded and cut
    into small dice
3 tablespoons/50 ml red wine vinegar
Extra-virgin olive oil

To finish
2 tablespoons olive oil
3 tablespoons/40 g butter
Extra-virgin olive oil, to serve

Pigeon (or squab) is not a game bird you often find in Portuguese restaurants, but it is served in some old *lisboeta* places. There, pigeons or partridges are typically cooked with onions, garlic, port, vinegar, and cinnamon, along with other spices. The richness and slightly sweet acidity, as well as the warmth of the cinnamon, offsets the gaminess of the pigeon beautifully. The longer it sits submerged in its juices after cooking, the better—even for up to a week. I like to enjoy it just above room temperature with plenty of crusty bread.

To marinate the squab — Put the squab in a bowl and cover with the oil, garlic, white wine, cinnamon stick, and bay leaves. Season with paprika, salt, white pepper, and black pepper. Leave to marinate in the fridge for a few hours.

To make the sauce — Heat 3 tablespoons/40 ml of the olive oil in a pan over medium heat. Add the onion, garlic, bay leaves, and cinnamon stick and cook gently until the onion is soft. Season with salt and white pepper. Add the carrots and red pepper and cook for a few minutes. Stir in the vinegar and the remaining 4 tablespoons/60 ml olive oil and cook gently until the red pepper is just soft. I like the carrots to be a little bit crunchy. Remove from the heat and leave to marinate while you cook the squab. Taste for seasoning after marinating and finish with an extra glug of extra-virgin olive oil.

To finish the dish — Preheat the oven to 390°F/200°C (convection 355°F/180°C). Remove the squab from the marinade and gently pat them dry. Heat the 2 tablespoons olive oil in a heavy-bottomed ovenproof pan over medium heat and add the squab, breast-side down. Cook evenly, turning them to get a golden color all over. Add the butter and, when it foams, use it to baste the squab. Transfer the squab, breast-side up, to the oven and roast for 10 to 12 minutes. (I prefer the meat to be pink. If you like it well done, cook for another 2 to 4 minutes.) Baste halfway through cooking. Remove the pan from the oven and let the squab rest for 5 minutes before serving. To serve, place the squab on the sauce and add a generous glug of extra-virgin olive oil.

Grilled cabbage with garlic butter and cannellini beans *Couve grelhada com feijão branco*

Serves 2

3½ ounces/100 g dried cannellini beans
   (or a 14-ounce/400 g can cannellini
   beans)
A pinch of baking soda
3 shallots, 1 halved, 1 sliced, and 1 diced
3 garlic cloves, 1 halved and 2 crushed
1 carrot, halved
1 stalk celery, cut into chunks
1 bay leaf
Flaky sea salt and ground white pepper
2 tablespoons/30 g butter
A small handful of parsley leaves,
   finely chopped
Freshly squeezed lemon juice
Smoked paprika
1 large sweetheart or napa cabbage
1 tablespoon olive oil

We love our beans in Portugal—fresh ones from the garden, as well as all kinds of dried beans that came to our shores from the New World. I prefer to use dried beans that I've soaked myself, but there's no problem with good-quality canned beans. The creamy flavor and fluffy texture of these beans are lovely with the garlic butter and smoky grilled cabbage. Lima beans would also work well.

If using dried beans, soak them overnight with the baking soda in plenty of water. Rinse and place in a pan with the halved shallot, halved garlic clove, carrot, celery, and bay leaf, and enough water to cover. Bring to a boil, skimming off any foam, and simmer for 45 minutes to 1 hour, or until tender (the cooking time will depend on the age of the beans). Remove from the heat and leave to cool in the cooking liquid. Season the cooking liquid while the beans cool.

Melt the butter in a pan over low heat. Add the crushed garlic and sliced shallot and cook gently for 5 minutes. Remove from the heat and set aside.

Drain the cooked or canned beans. Mix them together with the diced shallot, parsley, and a squeeze of lemon juice. Taste and season with salt, pepper, and paprika.

Preheat the oven to 390°F/200°C (convection 355°F/180°C). Remove the outer leaves from the cabbage and cut it in half lengthwise. Heat the olive oil in an ovenproof grill pan over high heat. Add the cabbage, cut-side down, season with salt and pepper, and roast for 3 minutes, or until caramelized. Turn it over and cook for 2 minutes on the other side. Add a splash of water, cover with foil, transfer to the oven, and roast for 5 minutes. Baste the cabbage with the garlic butter and roast for another few minutes. Remove from the oven and squeeze over a little lemon juice. I like to warm the cannellini beans through gently in the pan with the cabbage and then bring the pan to the table to serve.

Vinha d'alhos–style vegetables
Legumes com vinha d'alhos

**Serves 2 as a main course
or 4 as a side dish**

For the glaze

⅔ cup/150 ml red wine, ideally a
    light- to medium-bodied red
    wine such as a Pinot Noir

3 tablespoons/50 ml red wine vinegar,
    plus a little extra (optional)

3 tablespoons/50 ml freshly squeezed
    orange juice

3 garlic cloves, smashed

½ teaspoon toasted cumin seeds,
    gently crushed

2½ tablespoons/50 g honey

1 cinnamon stick

For the vegetables

3 red onions, cut into thick rings

14 ounces/400 g parsnips,
    halved lengthwise

17 ounces/500 g heirloom carrots,
    halved lengthwise

Flaky sea salt, ground white pepper,
    and cracked black pepper

1¾ ounces/50 g walnuts

3 slices day-old bread, such as ciabatta
    or sourdough

2 tablespoons olive oil

Finely grated zest of 1 orange

Finely grated zest of 1 lemon

A small handful of parsley leaves,
    finely chopped

Extra-virgin olive oil, to serve

Sadly, vegetables are often a bit of an afterthought in Portuguese gastronomy. They're often overcooked or added to stews that will be long simmered. Here, I've chosen to use vegetables that we know and love, giving them the *vinha d'alhos* (wine and garlic) treatment and resisting the temptation to add lots of meat. The result is this delicious roasted dish that can easily sit at the center of the table and hold its own.

To make the glaze — Put the glaze ingredients in a pan and cook over medium heat until the honey dissolves. Be careful not to reduce the glaze too much at this stage, as it will reduce further while cooking. Set aside.

To make the vegetables — Preheat the oven to 390°F/200°C (convection 355°F/180°C). Put the onions in a baking dish large enough to allow the vegetables plenty of room to roast, rather than steam (we want them to roast for flavor and color). Sit the parsnips and carrots on top of the onions and season with salt and white pepper. Pour the glaze over and mix well. Roast for 30 minutes, or until cooked through and golden brown. After 15 minutes, you can remove the cinnamon stick if you like (I prefer to leave it in). Baste the vegetables with the glaze two or three times while cooking. I also like to add an extra splash of red wine vinegar halfway through for an acidic kick.

Put the walnuts on a separate baking sheet and bake for a few minutes until lightly toasted. Coarsely chop them once cooled.

Make the croutons by tearing the bread into rough bite-size pieces. Heat the olive oil in a pan over medium heat, add the bread, and toast for 5 minutes, or until crispy and golden brown. Put the croutons in a bowl and mix in the orange and lemon zests and parsley. Season with salt and white pepper.

Once the vegetables are cooked, if the glaze seems too liquid you can simmer it in a pan to reduce, then spoon it back over the vegetables. Sprinkle the walnuts and croutons over the vegetables and add a generous glug of extra-virgin olive oil, flaky sea salt, and cracked black pepper.

Beach Life

Lisbon life in summer is tied to the beach. I don't think there's any other city in Europe that has such good beaches within striking distance, and that clarion call of sun, sea, sand, and seafood is hard for any *lisboeta* to resist. People finish work and jump in the car or onto the train to catch the last few hours of dying light beside the ocean—or phone in sick and hope the boss doesn't find out by seeing a picture of them out among the waves or flopping on a beach towel on social media. Surfing is huge in Lisbon, and many teenagers go through an obsessive phase. Even when we become adults, we never really shake it off—whether the surfboard is real or made from Styrofoam, we just run into the ocean and try to catch some waves. Yes, it's cold, but that doesn't stop us.

The closest good beach to Lisbon is Carcavelos, and in spite of its proximity to the city, it's pretty great. You just face the sea, turn a blind eye to the buildings behind you, and breathe in. The journey starts at the city's Cais do Sodré station, passes through Belém (famous for its *pastéis de nata*), and ends at the beach town of Cascais, with stops at a number of different beaches in between. The train gets really busy at Carcavelos, but the waters are clean because it sits at the mouth of the River Tejo.

Carcavelos is framed at one end by the majestic São Julião da Barra fortress, a sixteenth-century coastal defense complex that sits right on the headland. It is here that you should come if you want a taste of *lisboeta* beach bedlam at its best. You can walk along

the *paredão*, the sea wall that skirts along the series of little beaches like a promenade. In Estoril, you'll find the Casino Estoril, which featured in Ian Fleming's first James Bond novel *Casino Royale*—Fleming stayed in the town during the Second World War, operating as an MI5 agent. My grandparents owned a house in the area when I was young, and then later, when my parents split up, my father and I moved here too, so I spent many summer days and nights in and around Cascais and Estoril. When I'm passing through, I still like to go to Pastelaria Garrett for prawn *rissóis* (page 74), driven by childhood memories that make me crave these crescent-shaped pastries. Unlike the places that make a batch in the morning, then just leave them sitting on a plate for hours, here they fry their *salgados* (savory snacks) fresh throughout the day.

From Estoril, I like to walk on, past the lighthouses, fortresses, anchorages, and harbors, to my favorite beach: Praia do Guincho. It's two miles from Cascais and is a little harder to get to on public transport; perhaps that's why its wild and windy beauty is still so pristine. There's little beachside development here—just hills, cliffs, sand dunes, and stunning succulents. The air seems cleaner because you're far from the city, and I love to scoop up lungfuls of it, along with the smell of salt and seaweed. When I was younger, heading out to Guincho was always a gamble. Surf cams didn't exist then, so you never really knew what to expect from the weather until you got there,

but even on days when the sand whips up on your face, this place is always worth it. You'll often find people playing *jogar aos toques* (soccer kick ups). The Portuguese are really good at these fancy beach ball tricks, thanks to hours and hours of practice, and players will welcome you if you want to join in. Just say *Posso jogar?*—Can I play?

On a clear day, you can see the town of Sintra up on the pine-covered hills of the Serra de Sintra. This was once the retreat of Lisbon's elite—it's cooler up there—and it is filled with ostentatious, brightly colored palaces. We used to drive up in my grandfather's old Citroën just to get a packet of *queijadas de Sintra*, soft little cheesecakes that are almost as magical as the town itself. The cliff bends round to the headland of Cabo de Roca, the westernmost point on the European mainland. The Portuguese poet Luís de Camões wrote about it in his epic poem *Os Lusíadas*: "Here, where the land ends and the sea begins." Until the fourteenth century, people thought that this was the end of the world, and it's not hard to see why. Be careful when strolling along the edge here—the wind is dangerous.

Of course, the beach is not just about swimming or surfing in the freezing-cold Atlantic, or feeling the warmth of the sun on our bare skin, or teenage boys and girls partying. It's also about all the different foods we associate with it. *Bolas de Berlim* (page 42) are a quintessential part of beach life for *lisboetas*. These fat, sugary doughnuts are filled with

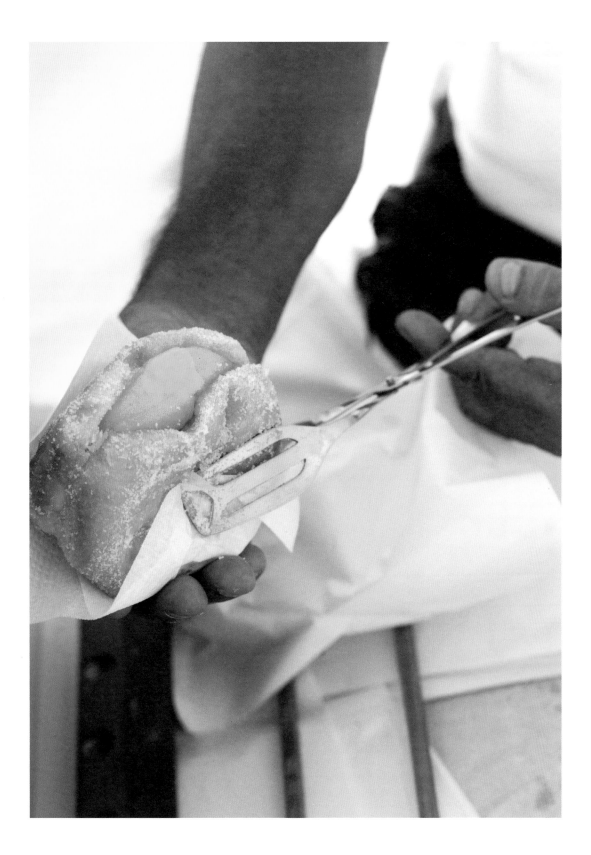

bright yellow cream that oozes from a slit on the side, and we love to eat them after a swim when the salt from the sea is drying on our lips and it mixes with the sugary dust. Sellers walk up and down the beach, crying out *Doughnuts!* and suddenly you want one. On Carcavelos I watch a doughnut seller called Miguel, dressed in white, as he advertises his wares with a shout: *Olha a bolinha! Bolas de Berlim!* I wave him over and he crouches down beside me, opening the white wooden box painted with Miguel dos Bolos in red letters that he carries on his shoulder. He opens it with some ceremony, and inside there are shelves stuffed with pastries. Taking a pair of metal tongs, he slides one into a fold of greaseproof paper. I bite into it and am transported back to my childhood. Another beach treat is *batatas fritas*—freshly made potato chips tossed in salt.

We don't go in for beach picnics much, though. Soggy sandwiches are not the thing when you can wander up to a beach shack and have a freshly made *bifana* (pork sandwich; page 280) or a plate of clams. But we do love picking *cadelinhas* (very small clams) on the water's edge and taking them home to cook. Across the bridge, on the Costa da Caparica, you'll see people at low tide standing in the shallows, spreading the toes of their bare feet into the sand looking for these tiny bivalves. Sometimes you have to be fast, because the surf will suddenly pull the shells back out to sea again. This chase is fun, and then when you have a bucketful of *cadelinhas*, you just leave them in saltwater to clean them out a bit. Later, you can steam them with garlic and cilantro and relish the fact that nature gave you this plate of deliciousness for free. On the rockier coastline around Cascais, you'll also see people crabbing, but this is a less rewarding sport—you are unlikely to find a crab big enough to eat, and when you do it'll be pretty good at nipping fingers. Nevertheless, kids love poking around pools in the hope of finding one.

Being a *lisboeta*, I am sentimental about the beach—it's a kind of *saudade*, a longing for endless, carefree days when you could run around almost naked. And when I get back to the beach, somehow, even if it is just for a few moments, I find myself feeling like that child again, and I am deliriously happy.

Kale migas with mushrooms
Migas de couve frisada e cogumelos

Serves 4

3 ounces/80 g white button mushrooms,
  thinly sliced
3 tablespoons/50 ml extra-virgin olive oil,
  plus extra to serve
Flaky sea salt and ground white pepper
Smoked paprika
5½ ounces/160 g Cornbead (page 299),
  sourdough, or other rustic loaf,
  cut into cubes
2 tablespoons olive oil
2 tablespoons rendered pork fat or lard
2 garlic cloves, crushed
A small bunch of cilantro, stalks
  and leaves finely chopped
3½ ounces/100 g kale, sliced

Migas is traditionally made from bread soaked in milk, which is then gently toasted in animal fat with lots of garlic and seasonal greens. The idea of eating soaked and fried bread may seem strange, but *migas* is fantastic. The bread base is a blank canvas that can take on other flavors—here I've used kale, cilantro, and garlic and added marinated mushrooms.

Put the mushrooms in a bowl. Pour on the extra-virgin olive oil, season with salt, pepper, and paprika, and stir. Set aside to marinate while you cook the *migas*.

Put the bread in another bowl and pour over boiling water to just cover it. Season with salt, pepper, and paprika, stir well, and set aside.

Heat the olive oil and pork fat in a pan over medium heat. Add the garlic and cilantro (reserving some cilantro leaves to garnish, if you like) and cook gently until fragrant. Increase the heat slightly, add the kale, and sauté for a few minutes until it starts to wilt. Add the soaked bread and cook for about 10 minutes, pressing it down with a spatula. As it cooks, move the bread around to incorporate it with the kale and let any liquid evaporate. When it crisps around the edges, turn it over and continue to cook until golden brown. The final texture should be crispy on the outside and soft inside.

Transfer to a serving dish and spoon the marinated mushrooms on top. Serve immediately.

Baked celery root with fennel and cilantro broth *Coentrada de funcho e raiz de aipo*

Serves 4

1 celery root, skin on
2 tablespoons olive oil
Flaky sea salt and ground white pepper

For the fennel broth
5 tablespoons olive oil
4 garlic cloves, crushed
A small bunch of cilantro, stalks and
    leaves finely chopped separately
Flaky sea salt and ground white pepper
1 large fennel bulb, trimmed and sliced
3½ cups/800 ml vegetable stock or water
Freshly squeezed lemon juice

Coentrada (literally "with cilantro") is a truly fantastic preparation. It has a similar flavor to some Chinese dishes: the acidity from the vinegar, the spice of white pepper, the strong fried garlic taste, the fragrance of the cilantro, and the lovely rich broth make the connection for me, and seem to demonstrate how Portugal's historical involvement with China has influenced Portuguese cooking. Although you can make this dish from start to finish on the same day, the fennel broth will have an even more beautiful flavor if you make it a day in advance.

Preheat the oven to 375°F/190°C (convection 340°F/170°C). Drizzle the celery root with the olive oil and season with salt and pepper. Wrap it in a loose parcel in foil, leaving space for it to steam. Put on a baking sheet and bake for 1 hour, or until cooked all the way through. Remove from the oven and allow to cool slightly before slicing. Cut into 8 pieces or wedges and set aside.

To make the fennel broth — Heat 3 tablespoons of the olive oil in a pan over low heat. Add the garlic and cilantro stalks, season with salt and pepper, and cook gently until fragrant. Add the fennel and cook gently for 10 minutes, or until soft. Pour in the stock, bring to a boil, then reduce the heat and simmer for 30 minutes. (This broth is also a very good base for soup: I like to blend it with a dash of cream to make a lovely fennel soup.) Remove the pan from the heat and stir in the chopped cilantro leaves, along with a dash of lemon juice.

Heat the remaining olive oil in a pan over medium heat. Add the celery root pieces, flesh side down, and cook on each side for 2 minutes, or until golden brown. Pour the broth into a serving dish with the celery root and serve.

Jerusalem artichokes and lacinato kale with garlic *Tupinambos e cavolo nero com alho*

Serves 4

⅔ cup/160 ml olive oil, plus extra
    for drizzling
1¾ ounces/50 g garlic cloves, peeled and
    left whole, plus 1 garlic clove, crushed
2 tablespoons light cream
14 ounces/400 g Jerusalem artichokes,
    halved lengthwise
Flaky sea salt and cracked black pepper
1½ ounces/40 g hazelnuts, toasted
    and chopped, optional
½ red chile, seeded and finely chopped
5 ounces/150 g lacinato kale, stalks
    discarded and leaves left whole
Freshly squeezed lemon juice (optional)

This is not a classic dish, but it uses a distinctive Portuguese "cooking language" and features our characteristically bold flavors. The confit garlic purée complements the rich, almost meaty flavors of the roasted Jerusalem artichokes beautifully and helps bind the dish together.

Heat the olive oil with the peeled garlic cloves in a small pan over low heat to about 180°F/80 to 85°C, or just below the simmering point, ensuring the garlic is fully submerged. Turn the heat down to its lowest possible setting. Confit gently for about 2 hours, or until the garlic is completely soft. Strain and reserve the oil (you can use any extra for cooking meat and fish, or for dressings). Using an immersion blender, purée the garlic with just enough of the oil to make a smooth paste, and stir in the cream. (I love this paste spread on toast with cheese, and it's also great with potatoes.)

Preheat the oven to 390°F/200°C (convection 355°F/180°C). Put the Jerusalem artichokes on a baking sheet, mix with 2 tablespoons of the garlic confit oil, and season with salt and pepper. Roast, cut-side down, for 30 minutes, or until golden brown.

Reduce the heat to 340°F/170°C (convection 300°F/150°C) and roast the hazelnuts for 10 to 12 minutes, or until golden brown. Once cooled, coarsely chop them.

Heat 2 tablespoons of the confit garlic oil in a pan over medium heat. Add the crushed garlic and chile with a little bit of salt and cook gently until soft. Increase the heat, add the kale, and sauté for a few minutes. Add a splash of water, cover, and steam for a few minutes until cooked through. Add the roasted Jerusalem artichokes and a drizzle of olive oil and cook for 2 minutes. Taste and season, adding a squeeze of lemon juice.

I like to spread a generous amount of garlic paste on each plate and put the artichokes and kale on top so that the vegetable juices combine with the garlic. You could also serve the garlic paste on the side. Sprinkle with the hazelnuts and serve.

Mushrooms with Alentejo-style chickpeas

Cogumelos com puré de grão à alentejana

**Serves 2 as a main course,
or 4 as a side dish**

For the chickpea purée
2 tablespoons olive oil
1 onion, diced
2 garlic cloves, crushed
Flaky sea salt and ground white pepper
Smoked paprika
7 ounces/200 g canned plum tomatoes
1 (14-ounce/400 g) can good-quality
    chickpeas, drained (liquid reserved);
    or 5½ ounces/160 g dried chickpeas,
    soaked and cooked as described on
    page 103 (cooking liquid reserved)
Freshly squeezed lemon juice
Extra-virgin olive oil, to serve

For the mushrooms
3 tablespoons olive oil
Flaky sea salt and ground white pepper
5 ounces/150 g whole portobello
    mushrooms
4 teaspoons/20 g butter
1 garlic clove, crushed
5 ounces/150 g oyster mushrooms
A splash of dry white wine
A small handful of parsley leaves,
    coarsely chopped
Freshly squeezed lemon juice

The mushroom season is much enjoyed in Lisbon and its restaurants. I have stuck to only a few varieties of mushrooms in this recipe, which means it can be made throughout the year, but if you try this during mushroom season, go crazy and sauté as many different mushrooms as you can find! The purée is based on another commonly used ingredient in Portuguese cooking: the lovely chickpea. It is super tasty and will almost certainly find its way into many other dishes in your kitchen.

To make the chickpea purée — Heat the olive oil in a pan over medium heat. Add the onion and cook for 10 minutes, or until soft. Add the garlic and cook for a few minutes, until fragrant. Season with sea salt, pepper, and paprika. Add the tomatoes and increase the heat to cook until caramelized. Look at the pan and see how the vegetables are reacting: you should hear them sizzling, not stewing, and you should start smelling the caramelization. Add the chickpeas and cook to toast them for a few minutes. Pour in ⅔ to ¾ cup/150 to 200 ml of the chickpea liquid and bring to a boil. Reduce the heat to low and simmer for 20 minutes, or until the chickpeas are starting to fall apart. Taste for seasoning and add a dash of lemon juice. Remove the pan from the heat and purée with an immersion blender. (I don't like a completely smooth texture, so I only blend it briefly.)

To cook the mushrooms — Heat the olive oil in a large frying pan over high heat. Season the mushrooms with salt and pepper. When the pan is hot, add the portobello mushrooms and cook for 3 minutes on each side, or until golden brown. Remove them from the pan. Reduce the heat to low, add the butter and garlic, and cook gently until soft and fragrant. Return the portobello mushrooms to the pan. Increase the heat to medium, then add the oyster mushrooms and cook quickly for a minute or two, basting them with the butter. Add the wine and cook for another minute. Remove the pan from the heat and stir in the parsley with a squeeze of lemon juice. Drizzle the chickpea purée with extra-virgin olive oil and a pinch of paprika and serve it alongside the mushrooms. Eat right away.

Potatoes with caramelized onions and melting cheese *Batatas à murro com cebola e queijo fundido*

Serves 4

14 ounces/400 g potatoes, such as
    Yukon gold or similar, skin on

2 garlic cloves, smashed

1 bay leaf

3 tablespoons olive oil

Flaky sea salt flakes, ground white pepper,
    and cracked black pepper

2 onions, thinly sliced

Sherry vinegar (optional)

3 ounces/80 g queijo da Serra, or another
    full-flavored soft cheese

This is a simple but lovely dish that combines three absolute Portuguese favorites: potatoes, onions, and cheese. If you can't find *queijo da Serra* cheese, try Époisses or Mont d'Or, or even grated Gruyère. If you happen to get hold of *queijo da Serra*, you may just want to increase the amount, depending on how much you love stinky, melting cheese. I sometimes eat a whole bowl of this, accompanied by nothing more than a glass of wine.

Cook the potatoes in a pan of boiling salted water until tender. Remove, drain, and allow to cool slightly. Preheat the oven to 430°F/220°C (convection 390°F/200°C). When the potatoes are cool to the touch, smash them lightly with your fist. Put them in an ovenproof dish with the garlic and bay leaf, pour 2 tablespoons of the olive oil on top, and stir to ensure they are thoroughly coated. Season with salt and white pepper and bake for 20 to 25 minutes, or until golden brown and crispy.

Meanwhile, heat the remaining oil in a pan over low heat, then add the onions and season with salt and white pepper. Cook gently for 10 to 15 minutes, or until very soft and translucent. To speed up the cooking process you can cover the onions with a cartouche. Create a cartouche by folding a square of baking parchment to make a thin triangle. Holding the triangle with the thin point over the center of the pan, cut the other end off so that is slightly longer than the radius of the pan. Unfold it, crumple it, and dampen it lightly with water, then place it on top of the onions and cover with a lid. When it's ready, try squeezing a piece of onion; it should be very soft and taste sweet. Increase the heat and let the onions caramelize and turn golden brown, stirring to stop them from sticking. Remove the cartouche and set aside. Add a splash of sherry vinegar for a little bit of acidity that cuts through the cheese.

Take the potatoes out of the oven and scatter the onions and spoon or scatter the cheese on top. Return the dish to the oven and cook until golden brown and bubbling. Remove from the oven and serve right away. I love to sprinkle a little cracked black pepper on top while it's hot.

Sobre

mesas

Eggs. I can hardly think of a Portuguese dessert that doesn't include them. Along with copious amounts of sugar, *ovos* are the main ingredients of *sobremesas*, the incredibly sweet creations that appear at the end of a large meal.

Some dessert recipes in Portugal date back hundreds of years to the Middle Ages, and many are Moorish in origin, but the birth of our sweet eggy desserts only truly occurred when cheaper sugar arrived in our country after the 1419 "discovery" of Madeira, where the crop could be grown successfully.

These celestial creations were the work of Portuguese nuns, who came up with recipes not only for puddings, but also for cakes and sweets made from—you guessed it—eggs and sugar. These were known as *doçes conventuais,* or convent sweets. Women were sometimes confined within the walls of God not because of a religious calling but due to social factors, so perhaps dreaming up elaborate confections was a delicious distraction from what I imagine might have been a dreary life. When religious orders were suppressed in 1834, the nuns continued these activities to raise money.

There are hundreds of recipes in the *doçaria conventual* repertoire, and they all echo with a story. As with *pastéis*, many have holy but fanciful names, such as *toucinho de céu* (bacon of heaven), which contains no bacon, funnily enough; it takes its name from the pork fat used in it and, I presume, the fact that it tastes like heaven. One of the recipes that follows is *pudim abade de Priscos* (Baked Egg and Lardo Custard with Port Caramel; page 259), named after the abbot of a town called Priscos in Braga province. My spin on the traditional recipe makes for a glossy yellow slice of goodness surrounded by a pool of wine-colored syrup. It really is a beauty.

Pão de ló (Egg and Olive Oil Cake; page 253) is one of my favorite desserts. Egg yolks, sugar, a touch of flour, and a nice, rich Portuguese olive oil come together to make a feathery sponge that stays gooey in the middle. I also strongly recommend trying *farófias* (page 260), which seemed like something from a fairytale when I was a child: fluffy meringues gently poached and served with fragrant milk.

Should the preponderance of eggs not be to your taste, try the lovely Drunken Figs with Pistachios and Cream (page 263) or the *bolo de bolacha* on page 270, an easy-to-make but delicious assembly of biscuits, coffee, and cream.

Rice pudding 250
Arroz doce

·

Egg and olive oil cake 253
Pão de ló

·

Baked custard with rice milk 254
Tigelada

·

Baked egg and lardo custard with port caramel 259
Pudim abade de Priscos

·

Floating poached meringues 260
Farófias

·

Drunken figs with pistachios and cream 263
Figos bêbados com pistachios e natas

·

Caramel walnut mousse 265
Baba de camelo

·

Layered caramel cream 266
Serradura

·

Angels' double chins 267
Papos de anjo

·

Biscuit cake 270
Bolo de bolacha

·

Caramel chocolate truffles 272
Brigadeiros

Rice pudding
Arroz doce

Serves 4

¾ cup/150 g short-grain white rice,
    preferably Portuguese Carolino,
    Japanese sushi, or Spanish Bomba rice
Flaky sea salt
3½ cups/800 ml whole milk
6 tablespoons/80 g superfine sugar
A couple of strips each of lemon and
    orange zest, plus grated zest (optional)
1 cinnamon stick, broken in half
3 egg yolks
3 tablespoons/50 ml light cream (optional)
1½ ounces/40 g pistachios, shelled,
    toasted, and coarsely chopped
Ground cinnamon

The enthusiasm for rice in Portugal knows no bounds, so it should be no surprise that we absolutely adore rice pudding. Whenever I cook this, the smell always takes me back to my childhood, when my grandmother used to make it. She would spread it out on a plate on the dining room table to cool down, and make patterns on the top with ground cinnamon. Most likely to avoid my continual pleas of *Is it ready yet?* she would always set a little bowlful aside for me to taste. In this recipe I have added pistachios to the classic plain version.

Rinse the rice according to the instructions on the package. Bring 1¼ cups/300 ml of water to a boil in a pan with a pinch of salt. Stir in the rice and cook over gentle heat for 15 minutes, or until the water is absorbed. Add a little extra water if it starts to stick.

Heat the milk and sugar in a separate pan with the lemon and orange zests and cinnamon stick. (I always count how many pieces of peel and cinnamon I put in the pan, which is helpful when I go fishing later to take them out.) Depending on how strong you want the flavors to be, you can remove the aromatics at this stage, or leave them in for a bit longer.

Pour the milk mixture into the rice gradually, stirring well after each addition. Continue to cook over low heat for another 20 minutes, or until thick and creamy. Just before serving, stir in the egg yolks and cream, and cook very gently for a couple of minutes. The rice will thicken as it cools, and you can adjust the consistency with a little extra cream or milk.

Serve the rice pudding in a large serving dish or individual bowls. I love to eat it with toasted pistachios and cinnamon sprinkled on top. You could also add a little extra grated lemon and orange zest.

Egg and olive oil cake
Pão de ló

Serves 4

½ cup/100 g superfine sugar

4 whole eggs plus 1 egg yolk

⅓ cup/80 ml olive oil

2 tablespoons/20 g all-purpose flour

Extra-virgin olive oil, to serve

Flaky sea salt, to serve

This is one of my favorite Portuguese desserts, which is made from just egg yolks, sugar, a touch of flour, and a rich Portuguese olive oil. The quantities here make quite a small cake, but they can easily be doubled or tripled.

Preheat the oven to 430°F/220°C (convection 390°F/200°C). Grease and line an 8-inch/20-cm round cake pan with baking parchment. Put the sugar, eggs, and yolk in the bowl of a stand mixer and beat for up to 30 minutes, until very light and fluffy.

Gently fold in the olive oil and flour and pour the batter into the pan. Bake for 8 minutes, or until the cake is just set but still a little gooey in the middle. Let it sit for 5 to 6 hours so that it collapses and sets, and the top forms a crust. Drizzle a generous glug of extra-virgin olive oil and add a sprinkle of sea salt on top, then eat it at room temperature.

Baked custard with rice milk
Tigelada

Serves 4 to 6

For the custard
Butter, for greasing
6 eggs
1 cup/200 g superfine sugar
5½ tablespoons/50 g all-purpose flour
A pinch of sea salt
2 cups/500 ml whole milk

For the rice milk
½ to ¾ cup/100 to 150 g short-grain
    white rice, preferably Portuguese
    Carolino, Japanese sushi, or
    Spanish Bomba rice
1 quart/1 L whole milk
6 tablespoons/75 g superfine sugar
1 cinnamon stick
A few strips each of orange and lemon zest
1 vanilla pod, split lengthwise
    (optional)

Flaky sea salt
Extra-virgin olive oil, to serve

Tigelada **means "cooked in a bowl," but in this case the custard is cooked in a baking dish. It is a simple combination of eggs, sugar, milk, and flour, which is whipped for a long time—it's best to use a stand mixer—and then baked. I like to serve this with rice milk on the side, scattered with a few drops of extra-virgin olive oil. Rice milk is a Portuguese take on** *horchata;* **you can also make a thinner version by taking out some of the rice before blending it, to serve over ice with a little** *aguardente velha* **(Portuguese brandy).**

To make the custard — Grease a 9 by 10-inch/23 by 25-cm baking dish with a thin layer of butter. Put the eggs, sugar, flour, and salt in the bowl of a stand mixer and whisk at medium speed until it nearly triples in volume and is pale and fluffy. It should leave a thick ribbon when you lift some up with a spoon. This will take around 30 minutes.

Turn the mixer speed down to low. Pour the milk into the bowl in a slow, steady stream and whisk for about 2 minutes, or until fully incorporated. Be careful at this stage not to overwork the mixture. Pour this custard mixture into the prepared baking dish, without going right to the top, and chill it in the fridge for an hour or so, uncovered.

To make the rice milk — Rinse the rice according to the package instructions. Put the rice in a pan with the milk, sugar, cinnamon stick, citrus zest, vanilla pod, and a pinch of sea salt. Cook over low heat for around 25 minutes, or until tender. Remove the cinnamon stick, citrus zest, and vanilla pod. (I always count the number of zest pieces I put in the milk so that when I'm fishing them out later I can catch them all.) There are a couple of options now: you can strain the milk to remove the rice and serve it as a drink, or blend some of the rice with the milk until smooth, depending on how thick you want it. You can pass it through a sieve after blending it. To serve it with *tigelada*, however, I normally blend a handful of the rice with the milk to get the consistency of light cream.

Preheat the oven to 480°F/250°C (convection 445°F/230°C). Bake the *tigelada* for 5 to 8 minutes, at which point it will start to expand and turn a golden-brown color. Reduce the oven temperature to 390°F/200°C (convection 355°F/180°C) and continue to cook for a further 15 minutes, or until set. Remove from the oven and leave to cool in the dish. You will notice that it will sink, but don't worry, this is normal. Serve in bowls with the rice milk alongside. Sprinkle a few drops of extra-virgin olive oil and a little sea salt onto the rice milk before serving.

Baked egg and lardo custard with port caramel *Pudim abade de Priscos*

Serves 4 to 6

For the port caramel
1¼ cups/250 g superfine sugar
3 tablespoons/50 ml ruby port

For the custard
2¼ cups/450 g superfine sugar
1 cinnamon stick
4 strips lemon zest
1¾ ounces/50 g sliced lardo
18 best-quality egg yolks

For the port sauce
2 cups/500 ml ruby port
1 slice orange
1 cinnamon stick
Sugar (optional)

Extra-virgin olive oil, to serve

This is my interpretation of a classic dessert. I have used the port, which is usually included in the custard, to make a flavorful syrup that offsets it beautifully. Pork fat is used in all kinds of Portuguese dishes, including desserts, and here it brings a lovely and rich—if unusual—flavor to the custard.

To make the port caramel — Heat the sugar in a pan with 7 tablespoons/100 ml of water. Once the sugar has dissolved, increase the heat and simmer gently to make an amber-colored caramel (it should reach 291°F/144°C). Carefully pour in the port. Pour the caramel into a baking dish or heatproof mold measuring about 8 inches/20 cm square and 2 inches/5 cm deep. Leave it to set in the fridge, preferably overnight.

To make the custard — Dissolve the sugar and 1 cup/250 ml of water in a pan over medium heat with the cinnamon and lemon zest. Cook gently to make a clear, light syrup (it should reach 233°F/112°C). Add the *lardo* and stir well until it melts. Strain the syrup through a heatproof sieve, then pour it slowly over the egg yolks in a heatproof bowl, whisking constantly. Pour the mixture into the mold over the set caramel and leave to rest for 30 minutes.

Preheat the oven to 300°F/150°C (convection 265°F/130°C). Cover the mold with foil, pricking the foil with a fork. Bake in a bain-marie for about 1 hour, or until the edges have set but it still wobbles in the middle. Remove from the oven and leave to cool until set in the middle (about 3 hours, or even until the next day). Loosen the edges with a knife and invert it onto a plate. If it doesn't come out, dip the mold briefly in hot water to loosen it.

To make the port sauce — Simmer the port with the orange slice and cinnamon stick for 15 minutes, until the alcohol has evaporated and it has reduced to a light syrup consistency. Scrape out any remaining caramel from the custard mold and strain it into the sauce. Taste and add a little sugar if needed. Set aside to cool.

To serve, cut the custard into slices and pour the cooled port sauce around it, then add a few drops of olive oil on top.

Floating poached meringues
Farófias

Serves 4

4 eggs, separated
¾ cup/150 g superfine sugar
3 cups/700 ml whole milk
1 cinnamon stick
2 strips orange zest
Ground cinnamon

Farófias **are our version of the French dessert** *îles flottantes* **(floating islands). The light meringues are gently poached in milk, which is then used as a base for a fragrant custard. The dessert should be eaten nice and cold with lots of ground cinnamon on top.**

Using a handheld electric mixer or whisk, whisk the egg whites to stiff peaks in a clean, dry bowl. Add ¼ cup/50 g of the sugar and whisk for another 2 minutes, until the mixture returns to stiff peaks and is thick and glossy, taking care not to overwhisk it.

Meanwhile, heat the milk in a pan over medium heat with the remaining ½ cup/100 g sugar, the cinnamon stick, and the orange zest. Poach the meringues in batches by dropping tablespoonfuls of the whisked egg whites into the milk. Cook for about 2 minutes, turning them gently with a spoon, until they puff up and look like little clouds. Transfer to a plate with a slotted spoon and set aside at room temperature.

Put the egg yolks in a bowl. Gradually pour the warm poaching milk onto the yolks, whisking continuously. Pour the mixture into the pan and cook over low heat, stirring, until it thickens to a light custard consistency. Be careful not to overheat it or the eggs may scramble. Pour the custard into a shallow bowl to cool, covered with plastic wrap to prevent a skin from forming.

Once cool, spoon the custard over the meringues and chill them before eating. Dust with cinnamon and serve cold.

Drunken figs with pistachios and cream
Figos bêbados com pistachios e natas

Serves 4

1⅛ cups/280 ml ruby port
⅓ cup/60 g superfine sugar
12 fresh figs
3 strips orange zest
1 cinnamon stick
1¾ ounces/50 g pistachios, shelled
7 tablespoons/100 ml heavy cream
7 tablespoons/100 g crème fraîche
1 teaspoon brandy, plus more to taste
Flaky sea salt (optional)

In Portugal we like to poach fruit in port, and figs are at the top of my list for this treatment. They have been grown in Portugal for centuries, as have pistachios. Use roasted green pistachios for this recipe if you can find them—they're my favorite.

Put the port in a large pan with the sugar and bring to a boil. Turn down the heat and simmer gently for 2 minutes. Add the figs, orange zest, and cinnamon, cover, and remove the pan from the heat. Leave to sit for 5 to 10 minutes, depending on how soft you want the figs to be.

Meanwhile, preheat the oven to 355°F/180°C (convection 320°F/160°C). Put the pistachios on a baking sheet and bake until lightly toasted. Once cooled, coarsely chop them.

Whisk the cream to soft peaks and fold in the crème fraîche. Stir in the brandy. Don't stir it too much at this stage or it may split. I like to add a little sea salt to the cream for a savory note.

Slice some of the figs in half and arrange these and the whole figs on a serving plate. Simmer the poaching liquid for a few minutes to reduce it to a glaze. Serve the figs with some of the glaze poured on top and a sprinkling of pistachios, with the brandy cream alongside.

Caramel walnut mousse
Baba de camelo

Serves 4 to 6

1 (14-ounce/397 g) can sweetened
     condensed milk or dulce de leche
4 eggs, separated
A pinch of sea salt
3½ ounces/100 g digestive biscuits
     (such as McVitie's), crushed
1¾ ounces/50 g toasted walnuts,
     coarsely chopped

The name of this dish literally means "camel's drool," which is weird, I know—it evokes something that you wouldn't really associate with desserts, or indeed with food in general. It's a great example of the Portuguese genius with condensed milk, and our ability to transform a humble and practical ingredient into a simple but utterly delicious dessert.

If you need to caramelize the condensed milk, put the can in a pan of warm water and bring to a boil over medium heat. It is important that the can is fully submerged. When the water comes to a boil, turn it down to a simmer. Simmer for 2 hours, rotating the can frequently; if you prefer a darker caramel, simmer it for 3 hours. Carefully remove the can and leave to cool before opening. (If you bought dulce de leche, you don't need to do this.)

In a large, clean bowl, whisk the egg whites to stiff peaks. In a separate large bowl, mix the condensed milk caramel with the egg yolks, whisking vigorously to incorporate them. To keep a nice airy texture, start by stirring in 1 tablespoon of the egg whites into the caramel to loosen the mixture, then gently fold in the rest of the egg whites, along with the salt. Be careful not to overmix or you will knock out the air. If you like, chill the mousse in the fridge for a few hours before assembling and serving (this helps tone down the sweetness a little bit).

Transfer to a serving bowl or individual glasses. Start with a layer of crushed biscuits and walnuts, then pour in the mousse and top with more biscuits and walnuts. If you want more texture, you can coarsely chop the walnuts and biscuits, or you can chop them to a fine crumb in a food processor. I like the biscuits to be quite fine and the walnuts chunky.

Layered caramel cream
Serradura

Serves 4 to 6

1 (14-ounce/397 g) can sweetened
    condensed milk or dulce de leche
⅞ cup/200 ml sugar syrup (page 33)
6 egg yolks
⅞ cup/200 ml whipping cream
8 ounces/250 g digestive or rich tea
    biscuits (such as McVitie's)

The unpromising name of this dessert—it literally means "sawdust"—comes from the texture of the ground biscuits as they are placed in layers between the caramel cream and egg custard. It results in a dessert rather like a layered mousse. *Serradura* would also make a lovely sundae if you froze the caramel cream and served it in scoops with the whipped cream and biscuit mixture.

If you need to caramelize the condensed milk, put the can in a pan of warm water and bring to a boil over medium heat. It is important that the can is fully submerged. When the water comes to a boil, turn it down to a simmer. Simmer for 2 hours, rotating the can frequently. Carefully remove the can and leave it to cool before opening. (If you bought dulce de leche, you don't need to do this.) Pour the cooled caramel into a large bowl and set aside.

Heat the sugar syrup in a pan until just boiling. Leave to cool for a few minutes. Put the egg yolks in a heatproof bowl and whisk lightly. Pour the sugar syrup over the yolks, whisking constantly. Pour the mixture back into the pan and cook gently over low heat for 10 to 12 minutes, stirring constantly, until thickened. Remove from the heat and transfer the egg cream to a plate to cool, covered with plastic wrap to prevent a skin from forming.

Whip the cream to soft peaks. Gently fold the whipped cream into the caramel.

You can serve this in one large bowl or in individual bowls or glasses. Start with a layer of egg cream on the bottom, then a layer of the caramel cream. Sprinkle with the crushed biscuits, follow with another layer of caramel cream and biscuits, and finally finish with a layer of egg cream and biscuits.

Angels' double chins
Papos de anjo

Serves 4

Butter, for greasing

Flour, for dusting

1¼ cups/250 g superfine sugar

1 cinnamon stick

1 strip orange zest

1 strip lemon zest

1 vanilla pod, split lengthwise

A splash of aguardente velha,
    cognac, or aged dark rum

12 egg yolks

2 eggs

2 tablespoons/15 g cornstarch

These little syrup-soaked cakes can be found all over Lisbon. They are rather rich, so I usually prefer to eat them when they are cold, which tones down the sweetness. Here I have reduced the amount of sugar in the syrup and in the cakes, as this allows the other flavors to shine. They are nice served with whipped cream flavored with a little bit of alcohol, such as *aguardente velha* or brandy.

Preheat the oven to 390°F/200°C (convection 355°F/180°C). Grease a 12-hole muffin pan with butter and dust it with flour.

First, make a sugar syrup: Heat 1 cup/250 ml of water with the sugar, cinnamon stick, and orange and lemon zests. Scrape the vanilla seeds into the pan and add the pod. When the sugar has fully dissolved, increase the heat and boil for 2 minutes. Take the pan off the heat and set aside to infuse for at least 30 minutes, ideally for 1 hour. Strain. This syrup is quite sweet and, once cooled, I like to dilute it with about 7 tablespoons/100 ml of water (to taste) and add a splash of *aguardente* to it.

Put the egg yolks, eggs, and cornstarch in the bowl of a stand mixer and beat at medium-high speed for about 20 minutes, or until the mixture leaves a ribbon trail when you lift some up with a spoon. Pour the mixture into the muffin pan and bake for 10 minutes, or until set. Leave the cakes to cool slightly, then gently remove them from the pan.

Prick the bottoms of the cakes with a fork and dip them in and out of the sugar syrup quickly. Spoon some syrup on top of the cakes, taking care not to submerge them. Put them in the fridge and leave them to sit for a couple of hours before serving.

Biscuit cake
Bolo de bolacha

Serves 4 to 6

⅞ cup/200 ml sugar syrup (page 33)
6 egg yolks
17 ounces/500 g rich tea biscuits
1 double espresso mixed with
    7 tablespoons/100 ml water, or
    ⅔ ounce/20 g instant coffee mixed
    with 7 tablespoons/100 ml water
1¾ ounces/50 g toasted walnuts,
    roughly chopped (optional)

This is basically a cookies-and-cream cake, the kind that kids love to drive a giant spoon into. In Portugal we use *bolacha Maria* cookies, which are similar in flavor and texture to rich tea biscuits (such as McVitie's). Many people use a buttercream filling, but I prefer a custardlike egg cream, which is not as heavy and less sweet. The nuts are optional, but I enjoy them.

Heat the sugar syrup in a pan until just boiling, then leave to cool for a few minutes. Put the egg yolks in a heatproof bowl and whisk lightly. Pour the sugar syrup over the yolks, whisking constantly. Pour the mixture back into the pan and cook gently over low heat for 10 to 12 minutes, stirring constantly, until thickened. Remove from the heat and transfer to a plate to cool, covered in plastic wrap to prevent a skin from forming.

Build the cake on the plate or tray you will serve it on. Dip the biscuits in and out of the coffee quickly and arrange them in a circle with one in the middle and six surrounding it. Spread a layer of egg cream on top and sprinkle with walnuts. If you find the egg cream is a little thick for your liking, you can dilute it with a few drops of cold coffee. Continue building up the layers of biscuits, egg cream, and walnuts until you have used all the biscuits. Spread a thin layer of the egg cream over the outside of the cake and a final sprinkle of walnuts on top. Chill in the fridge for a couple of hours before serving.

Caramel chocolate truffles
Brigadeiros

Makes about 15

1 (14-ounce/397 g) can sweetened
    condensed milk or dulce de leche
14 ounces/400 g dark chocolate,
    minimum 70 percent cocoa solids
1 tablespoon cocoa powder
⅞ cup/200 ml heavy cream
A pinch of fine sea salt

Brigadeiros **are the Portuguese version of chocolate truffles. Condensed milk is often used in Portuguese desserts, and it can be bought precaramelized as dulce de leche; if possible, try to avoid the brands that have very high sugar contents.**

If you need to caramelize the condensed milk, put the can in a pan of warm water and bring to a boil over medium heat. It is important that the can is fully submerged. When the water comes to a boil, turn it down to a simmer. Simmer for 2 hours, rotating the can frequently. Carefully remove the can and leave to cool before opening. (If you bought dulce de leche, you don't need to do this.)

Meanwhile, chop 7 ounces/200 g of the chocolate and put it in a bowl with the cocoa powder. Heat the cream in a small pan to just below the boiling point, then pour it gradually over the chocolate, mixing well after each addition. When the chocolate has melted and the mixture is smooth and glossy, fold in the caramelized condensed milk and the salt. Refrigerate the mixture for 2 to 3 hours or freeze for 20 minutes before shaping: it should be firm but still pliable.

To shape the *brigadeiros*, you need to work on a cold surface; my hands are always warm, so I keep everything else very cold when making them. Finely grate half the remaining 7 ounces/200 g chocolate and coarsely grate the rest, mix it together, and then spread it out on a sheet pan or large plate. Use a teaspoon to scoop up the chocolate caramel mixture and roll it gently into balls with your hands. Roll the balls in the grated chocolate to coat them completely. If the mixture starts to get too soft, put it in the freezer for a few minutes.

The *brigadeiros* will keep in the fridge for 3 days in an airtight container, or you can freeze them for 1 month. You could add different coatings, such as crushed pecans, pistachios, walnuts, dried coconut, or candied orange peel.

San

des

We don't often have sandwiches for lunch in Portugal. In fact, you might be delighted to know that instead we eat them as a late-night snack— really, we do! I honestly don't think you can beat a Portuguese *bifana* (pork sandwich) or *prego* (steak sandwich) when they're good. I'm emphasizing that word here, because for a sandwich to be good you need good components: bread, butter, meat, marinade, and sauce.

The *bifana* is like a superior version of a burger, and you'll find it served across Lisbon in late-night food trucks, cafés, and *tascas*. It's the perfect example of how flavors and textures can combine to bring something truly momentous to your mouth. There's a crusty roll, sometimes warmed through or toasted, stuffed with a slice of pork that has been marinated in *massa de pimentão* (red pepper paste) and simmered long and slow in a mysterious sauce.

Our next most famous sandwich is the *prego*: a tender piece of beef that's flash-fried, crammed into a roll, and drenched in cheap, sweet, bright yellow mustard. In the *cervejarias* (beer houses) and *marisqueiras (*shellfish restaurants) where *lisboetas* feast on seafood, the meal is often finished off with a *prego*.

Our national triumvirate of sandwiches is completed by *sandes de leitão*, in which crackling-covered suckling pig is stuffed into a roll and doused with peppery gravy. I haven't included a recipe in this chapter because it's highly unlikely you'll spit-roast your own little pig, but do grab one of these when you come to Portugal.

All of these sandwiches are eaten with your hands, the bread held with one of those cheap, thin paper napkins you can practically spit peas through. Most of them are inexpensive to buy in Lisbon and aren't too expensive to make at home, but I have included an indulgent creation of my own: the Prawn Sandwich with Garlic on page 289, which takes the "dirty" of the traditional sandwiches and kicks it up a notch. I use large prawns, which are plentiful in Portugal but still pretty expensive, so this is a luxurious treat.

I have given you some recipes for bread and rolls so that you can create extra-delicious sandwiches, but of course you can just make them with what you have around. Whatever you use, toast the bread rolls in a pan on the stovetop, or under the broiler (I like to use the same pan I cooked the steak, pork, or prawn filling in). I only toast the cut side of the roll, which results in a lovely contrast between crisp and soft—the perfect texture when you tuck in.

In other words, these are no run-of-the-mill sandwiches, but definitely worth the extra effort. A good sandwich is not just some fridge fluff to be eaten on the run—it is to be utterly relished.

Pork sandwich with chouriço butter 280
Bifana

·

Steak sandwich 283
Prego

·

Sweet potato rolls 286
Bolos do caco

·

Prawn sandwich with garlic 289
Sandes de gambas ao alho

·

Squid sandwich with lemon aioli 290
Sandes de choco grelhado

·

Chouriço walnut rolls 292
Pão com chouriço

·

Blood sausage and apple sandwich 297
Sandes de morcela com maçã

·

Cornbread 299
Broa

·

Eggplant and zucchini piso rolls 300
Sandes de beringela e courgette com piso

Pork sandwich with chouriço butter *Bifana*

Serves 2

2 (5-ounce/150 g) thin pork shoulder steaks
7 tablespoons/100 g red pepper paste
    (page 173)
1 tablespoon olive oil
2 Sweet Potato Rolls (page 286)
    or soft bread rolls

For the chouriço butter
4 tablespoons/60 g butter
4 tablespoons/60 g Ibérico pork fat
    or first quality lard
1 ounce/35 g chouriço (skin removed),
    finely diced
1 bay leaf
1 garlic clove, smashed

The *bifana* is the Portuguese equivalent of a burger—the best, most craved sandwich in the country. Ask your butcher for the most flavorful pork steaks he or she has, such as shoulder, and slice them thinly. The steaks are marinated overnight in red pepper paste, which makes the meat extremely tender, and a bit of *chouriço* butter is the finishing touch. The recipe below makes a little more than you'll need, but any extra can be used to dress grilled vegetables (try broccoli or zucchini), or melted over roast potatoes.

Using a small, sharp knife, score the pork steaks lightly in a crisscross pattern (this helps the pork absorb the marinade). Put them on a plate and cover both sides evenly with the red pepper paste. Cover loosely with plastic wrap and leave to marinate in the fridge for 8 hours, or ideally overnight.

To make the chouriço butter — Melt the butter and pork fat in a small pan over medium heat. Stir in the *chouriço* and cook for a few minutes until crispy. Add the bay leaf and garlic, take it off the heat, and leave to cool (adding the aromatics at this stage means they don't become overpowering). When the butter has set, remove the bay leaf and garlic. Scrape the butter out onto baking parchment, wrap it, and chill in the fridge until needed. Use within 1 week.

Allow the *chouriço* butter to come to room temperature. Heat the olive oil in a frying pan over medium-high heat. Once hot, add the pork and cook for 3 minutes on each side, or until golden brown. Add a little *chouriço* butter and use it to baste the meat. Remove the steaks and leave them to rest on a warm plate.

Cut the bread rolls in half and toast them on the cut side in the same pan. Thinly slice the pork. Spread the *chouriço* butter on the rolls, fill them with pork, and eat immediately.

Steak sandwich

Prego

Serves 2

2 tablespoons Ibérico pork fat or
    first quality lard

2 (5-ounce/150 g) minute steaks, such as
    thinly sliced sirloin, flank, skirt, or
    hanger steak

Flaky sea salt and cracked black pepper

2 tablespoons olive oil

1 tablespoon butter

2 Sweet Potato Rolls (page 286)
    or soft bread rolls

4 thin slices Ibérico ham

8 thin slices lardo

A few leaves of fresh sorrel
    or some lemon juice (optional)

Piri piri oil (page 156), to serve

Portuguese-style mustard (see page 20),
    to serve

A *prego* is a tasty steak sandwich found on every corner in Lisbon: a minute steak seasoned with salt, pepper, bay leaf, and garlic in a fresh bread roll. I fondly remember eating them on many long nights out in the bohemian districts of Old Lisbon, where the steak is usually cooked in a scorching-hot pan with some sort of animal fat. Properly made, it's a work of art that will feed the stomach and the soul, and here you have the *prego* of my dreams, with lots of ham and *lardo*. Make sure every single ingredient is as good as it can be; in Portugal we use *bolos do caco* (sweet potato rolls), but a soft white roll is a good alternative. You'll need to allow at least 6 hours for marinating.

Rub the pork fat over the steaks, ensuring they are fully covered. Leave to marinate in the fridge for 6 hours, or ideally overnight.

Take the steaks out of the fridge at least 20 minutes before cooking; they should have absorbed most of the pork fat, but you can rub off any excess with a paper towel (I like to leave it on for extra flavor). Season them well on each side with salt and pepper.

Heat the olive oil in a frying pan over high heat. When the pan is very hot, add the first steak and cook for 2 minutes on each side, then remove and repeat with the other one. While cooking, add the butter and use it to baste the steak. Take care not to overcook the steaks; they should still be juicy. Transfer them to a warm plate and leave to rest.

Cut the rolls in half. Toast the rolls, cut-side down, over medium heat in the same pan, so they absorb the cooking juices. Just before serving, slice the steaks to fit the rolls. Put a couple of slices of Ibérico ham in each roll, followed by slices of steak, then some *lardo* and a twist of cracked black pepper. Spoon any leftover cooking juices on top. You could also add some chopped fresh sorrel or a squeeze of lemon juice for an acidic kick, along with piri piri oil and Portuguese mustard. Serve right away.

Santo António

One of my favorite moments of the year is June 12, the night before the *festa de Santo António*. It's part of a city-wide carnival of dancing, singing, and marching, and at the heart of it all is some incredible food.

This big party marks the beginning of summer for me, and it's always tied up with the smell of sweet sardines being grilled in the streets of Old Lisbon. The whole city is covered in smoke, and some sources claim that thirteen sardines are eaten per second throughout that night. When the days get longer and warmer, these small but beautiful fish start to come back into season, and we can't wait to get our first taste of the good ones. They're caught not far from our Atlantic beaches, and between June and late September we devour them. I think a passion for sardines is in the Portuguese blood, and for us, the fattier the fish are, the better.

During Santo António, you'll see people who've never set foot in a professional kitchen tending their charcoal grills brilliantly, managing to cook their fish to perfection, adding salt and steam and deftly working their tongs, engulfed in the vapors. The name of a person who tends a grill like this is an *assador*, but I like to think of them as *sardinistas* because of the skill it takes to produce hundreds of amazing sardines one after the other all night long. We love *sardinha no pão*, in which the fish are piled on top of rustic bread that absorbs all the lovely juices and oils. Sardines are traditionally served with a salad of charred and peeled green peppers, lots

of thinly sliced sweet onions, and garlic and cilantro made glossy with plenty of extra-virgin olive oil.

All across the city, you'll find people with an eye to making some easy cash who have set up grills made from oil drums, metal barrels, trash cans, even car wheels. Right on the street, they pull out tables and chairs from their houses and run their own little alfresco restaurants. Living room windows are thrown wide open and owners hang out of them selling plastic glasses of wine for one euro. People get kegs and stand there on the cobblestones, pouring out the small beers we call *imperials*. Others mix up pitchers of sangria made with wine, fruit, soda, and sometimes brandy or vodka. They pin handwritten price lists on the wall beside their front door and sell drinks by the hundreds. I love these small-scale wheeler-dealers, and imagine them taking their profit and going out and buying a big TV or getting a better car. We call them *desenrascados*: wise guys or girls with their eye on the money. The Portuguese spirit is fast and, given our country's still feeble economy, getting out on the streets and selling things that add to the party is pretty clever.

Santo António is a real community party, when old people will drag out their comfy armchairs and sit with a drink, babies sit up on daddy's shoulders or are pushed in strollers, and little kids run around. I wish I could be here every year with my family so that they could enjoy the part of them that is Portuguese and feel

that pride as it pulses through all the people nearby. I'd show them how all the different neighborhoods come together, decorate their streets, and celebrate the city's saint. These are local gatherings that we call *arraiais*, and they can be anything from a cluster of plastic tables and chairs to an almost professional event run by a community association. In the streets of the old city, particularly in the tight warrens and alleyways of Alfama, our city's medieval Moorish quarter, Santo António is madness, and you might lose your friends, and possibly your sanity. But it's easy to seek out a calmer vibe in places like Madragoa, where there's not so much elbow jostling or hustle and bustle.

People drift from one neighborhood to the next looking for the best *sardinhada* (sardine party). Because the sardine is a beautiful but cheap fish, almost everyone can afford to take part in the celebrations and eat lots of them—this is definitely not an expensive night out. These days, there's little religion involved in the *festa de Santo António*, and I suspect we celebrate it on the eve of the actual saint's day with the hangover in mind, as it's a public holiday on June 13. You do see statues of Santo António everywhere you go in the city at this time, though—shops, bars, living rooms, and street corners have their own figurines, some of them homemade.

When we are at school, *lisboetas* are told the story of Fernando Martins de Bulhões, a child born to affluent parents in Alfama in the early twelfth century. At the age of nineteen, he joined a monastery against the will of his father; his rebellion is very much something I recognize because I left Lisbon and my own family at the same age. Eventually Fernando became a Franciscan friar in Italy and adopted the name António. At school our teacher told us how Santo António gave a sermon in Padua, but the heretics wouldn't listen to him. Disillusioned, the young friar went to the river and started preaching, and, the story goes, the fish came out to listen. I remember seeing one of our beautiful Portuguese tiled frescos, painted in blue and white, with hundreds of fish popping out of the water and tilting their heads to one side so they could hear the sermon better. I laugh at the thought now, because years of cutting and cooking fish has taught me many things, one of which is that fish don't have ears. They can hear, but not at all well. To me, the story of the sermon at Padua is a bit far-fetched, but it makes sense that Santo António went on to become the unofficial patron saint of fishermen—and, of course, of his birthplace.

The day of Santo António has its own traditions, and the biggest of these are the *marchas populares de Lisboa*, parades in which each neighborhood of the city competes in a kind of marching-meets-dancing competition. For months before the event, local people of all ages gather in halls to rehearse dance routines and marching steps; they'll learn songs, even writing some, and seamstresses will spend long evenings sewing up this

year's elaborate costumes, praying that they'll win the prize and bring it back home to the neighborhood party waiting for them. There's a carnival procession in front of dignitaries—the prime minister, the president, and the mayor—and grandstands along the roadside are filled with *lisboetas* and tourists, cheering them on.

In Bica, right in the heart of Old Lisbon, I watch this area's *march-antes* get ready for the parade. The marchers have gathered on some steps—Bica, which takes its name from a water fountain, is one of the steepest neighborhoods in a very steep city—and I arrive just as they're making last-minute adjustments to elaborate and, I have to tell you, quite lurid costumes made from Day-Glo polyester and netting. I head to Calçada da Bica Grande, a street of steps that runs parallel to the Elevador de Bica (the funicular that has been running up and down the hill since 1892). There I watch a woman, one of dozens all over the city doing the same thing, with tape measures draped around her neck as she rummages in a bag filled with ribbons, sequins, and glue. She probably made these outfits and wants everything to be perfect before she'll let them go into the competition. She straps young women into their corsets and checks their hair and makeup, and I see her smile at her work. This last-minute finessing adds to the buildup, and I can feel the buzz bubbling up all around me.

Everywhere the streets are hung with paper lanterns and garlands in a kaleidoscope of colors, and fairy

lights loop down from balconies and railings. I look up and notice aworn Portuguese flag pinned up below a window, probably put there more than a decade ago. The next window along sports a brand new flag, the red and green shouting proud and making me remember what it was like to grow up in Portugal during the "hardship days," when things were really tough and the country was in crisis. Santo António was a much more somber day back then, and people binge drank, more to drown their sorrows than to celebrate. But these days that's not the case—all around me, I see Portuguese pride and *lisboetas* with a newfound energy, and I love that.

The last ribbons tied, the headresses—which resemble caravels, the boats of the Portuguese Discoveries—fixed in place with bobby pins, the marchers from different parts of the city head up to their assembly point at Praça Marquês de Pombal before parading down Avenida de Liberdade, our biggest street, and into the old city. Rivalry is fierce, especially between Alfama and Castelo, and each year there are vicious accusations of a "fix," because somehow Alfama seems to win all the time.

Santo António is said to be the saint of lost things, but people also believe he brings luck to marriages, and every year his saint day features a peculiar event known as the *noivas de Santo António* (brides of Saint Anthony), at which Lisbon couples hope for the best of luck by taking their vows at a mass wedding in Sé Cathedral. This tradition started back in the late 1950s, when money was tight, so couples were helped by the city to get married. It was banned for a few years following the 1974 revolution, but eventually brides and grooms started reappearing to celebrate their nuptials together and, every year, you'll see them being showered with confetti and rice on the cathedral steps after they've tied the knot.

These are not the only romantics in the city on this day. Everywhere you'll see people selling pots of *manjerico* (bush basil) on the pavement, each with a paper flower and a little flag with a *quadra* (love poem). These are traditionally given as gifts by young men to their girlfriends, and nowadays friends often buy them for each other too. This pure act of offering something so nice to a friend makes me smile, and I can't help doing the same, buying half a dozen for my buddies. *Manjerico* came to Portugal from India, and it has a fresher, more intensely green aroma than traditional, larger-leaved basil—rub it gently, then smell your fingers; don't sniff the plant itself, because, according to folklore, this will cause it to die. I buy an extra one for my Lisbon kitchen. Portuguese people laugh at the idea of cooking with *manjerico*, but I think it's just something they haven't considered before. It's a fantastic aromatic to use, because its flavor really is refreshing, and marries beautifully with sardines.

If I'm in town for the big party, I love to catch up with friends and seek out not only sardines but also a

good *bifana* (pork sandwich; page 280), which is one of my favorite sandwiches in the world. On my last pilgrimage to Santo António, I ran into my great friend Miguel Pires, a food writer and true gourmet. He knows all that is exceptional about Portuguese food— how to cook it and how to find it. We searched the streets for the best *bifana*, and our noses led us to a guy who was making really fantastic ones in his kitchen—we had to lean in through his window to buy them, so we got a great view of how he was cooking them. Instead of just frying or grilling his pork, he simmered it in the juices in the pan, the meat bubbling in a *molho*, a sauce lush with pork fat, olive oil, wine, garlic, bay leaf, and *massa de pimentão* (fermented red pepper paste). Unlike other, cheeky pavement vendors who would have cooked the meat beforehand, this old guy was making them to order. Even though we had to wait a while, it was worth it, and the taste of that *bifana* will stay with me for quite some time.

Another food synonymous with Santo António is *caldo verde*, which is a national gastronomic treasure. It's a soup of finely shredded *couve galega* (cabbage) and potatoes, made rich and addictive by the addition of sweet, smoky *chouriço*. When *lisboetas* party, we always find a spot in our tummies for a warm bowl of *caldo verde* to carry us through the rest of the night and into the morning.

At around nine or ten o'clock, all the *marchantes* return to their own neighborhoods, eat some food, and really get into the swing. DJ booths are stuck up on people's balconies and temporary scaffolding is erected, and everywhere speakers are booming out "Cheira bem, cheira Lisboa," a song we love by the famous Portuguese singer Amália Rodrigues. "It smells good, it smells of Lisbon," she sings, and we all join in.

Miguel and I decide to follow our feast with a plate of *arroz doce*, a sweet, creamy rice pudding spiced with cinnamon and lemon zest and usually associated with Christmas, but loved so much by the Portuguese that we'll use any excuse to eat it. Our last stop is at a stall piping out *farturas*, which are Portugal's version of Spain's *churros* or America's funnel cakes, amazing air-filled tubes of *choux* dough scented with lemon, deep-fried and then rolled in sugar and cinnamon. Sorry, my Spanish friends, but they're much better than *churros*.

You really must visit Lisbon during Santo António. It's a great time to peel back the layers of my beautiful, ancient city. I promise you'll be hypnotized by the fantastic sights and smells as *lisboetas* revel in this glorious night and day in the city of light.

Sweet potato rolls
Bolos do caco

Makes 6 to 8

6 ounces/180 g (about 1 medium)
    sweet potato
1 teaspoon/5 g active dried yeast
4 teaspoons/20 g superfine sugar
2 tablespoons/30 g butter, melted
3⅓ cups/475 g bread flour, plus extra
    for dusting
1 teaspoon/5 g fine sea salt
1 teaspoon olive oil, plus extra for greasing

Bolos do caco are flat and muffin-like bread rolls—*bolo* means "cake" and *caco* means "broken piece," which refers to the stones that they would once have been baked on. The recipe originally came from Madeira, where sweet potatoes are grown extensively, and their lovely roasted flavor adds its own complexity to the bread. In Portugal, *bolos do caco* are often used for hot sandwiches such as *bifana* or *prego* (pages 280 and 283), and they're also good with garlic or brandy butter.

Preheat the oven to 410°F/210°C (convection 375°F/190°C). Wrap the sweet potato in foil, put it on a baking sheet, and bake for around 45 minutes, or until soft. Remove and leave to cool, then peel and mash the potato with a fork, or use an immersion blender to purée it until smooth.

Dissolve the yeast in a small bowl with 1 teaspoon/5 g of the sugar in 3 tablespoons/50 ml warm water. Leave it to stand for a few minutes until it starts to foam on top. Put the sweet potato, melted butter, flour, salt, and the rest of the sugar in the bowl of a stand mixer. Pour in the yeast mixture and 7 tablespoons/ 100 ml of water and mix, using the dough hook, for 8 minutes, or until smooth. Transfer the dough to a lightly oiled bowl and cover it with a kitchen towel. Leave it to rise in a warm place for about 1 hour, or until it has doubled in size.

Line a baking sheet with baking parchment and lightly dust it with flour. Turn the dough out onto a lightly floured work surface. Divide it into 6 equal pieces and roll each piece into a ball. Press each one down slightly with the back of your hand. Place the rolls on the prepared baking sheet, cover with a kitchen towel, and leave to rise for 30 to 45 minutes, or until they start to puff up.

Preheat the oven to 410°F/210°C (convection 375°F/190°C) and put a wire rack on the middle shelf of the oven. Brush the olive oil over a large ridged grill pan and heat it over medium-high heat. Once hot, add the rolls in batches of 2 or 3 at a time and cook, pressing down on each one, so that they end up about 1½ inches/ 4-cm thick. Cook for 3 minutes on each side, until golden brown. Transfer to the oven and bake directly on the wire rack for 10 more minutes. Transfer to a second wire rack and leave to cool.

Prawn sandwich with garlic

Sandes de gambas ao alho

Serves 2

12 large tiger prawns, raw (preferably)
    or cooked
Flaky sea salt and ground white pepper
A pinch of smoked paprika
2 tablespoons olive oil
1 teaspoon butter
1 garlic clove, crushed
½ small long red chile, seeded
    and thinly sliced
2 Sweet Potato Rolls (page 286), ciabatta,
    or soft bread rolls
A handful of arugula and watercress
A few cilantro leaves, coarsely chopped
1 teaspoon extra-virgin olive oil
Freshly squeezed lemon juice

Seafood was always a treat when I was young—sometimes we'd share a plate of prawns at the kitchen table, and each person was allowed just one. The idea of serving a large portion of these super-juicy prawns with buttery garlic, chile, and cilantro soaking onto a soft roll is the ultimate treat.

If you are using raw prawns, ask your fishmonger to peel and devein them, keeping the prawns whole. Season the prawns, whether raw or cooked, with salt, pepper, and paprika.

Heat the olive oil and butter in a frying pan over medium heat, then add the garlic and chile and cook for 1 minute, or until fragrant. Add the prawns, stir well, and cook for a couple of minutes. If using cooked prawns, be careful not to overcook them or they will turn rubbery. If using raw prawns, you may need to cook them for an extra 1 to 2 minutes, until cooked through. Take the pan off the heat and transfer the prawns, with the cooking juices, to a plate.

Cut the rolls in half and toast them cut-side down in the same pan for a couple of minutes. In a small bowl, season the green leaves and cilantro with extra-virgin olive oil, salt, pepper, and lemon juice. Put the prawns on the bottom half of the roll and the salad on top. Spoon any extra cooking juices over and eat immediately.

Squid sandwich with lemon aioli
Sandes de choco grelhado

Serves 2

For the lemon aioli
2 egg yolks
Flaky sea salt and ground white pepper
1 teaspoon Dijon mustard
7 tablespoons/100 ml grapeseed oil
7 tablespoons/100 ml olive oil
1 garlic clove, crushed
White wine vinegar
Freshly squeezed lemon juice

For the sandwich
2 tablespoons olive oil, plus
    a little extra if needed
1 small white onion, thinly sliced
Flaky sea salt and ground white pepper
1 squid tube (about 8 ounces/250 g),
    cleaned
4 slices rye or sourdough bread
A handful of arugula leaves

Squid makes an excellent sandwich. The key is to cook it at the last minute, just before eating, and to be careful not to overcook it. Here it is paired with caramelized onions and a lemony aioli. Eat your squid sandwich outdoors on a sunny day with a lovely glass of Portuguese white wine.

To make the lemon aioli — Put a bowl on a damp cloth to hold it steady. Add the egg yolks with a pinch of salt and the mustard, then beat for 1 minute, until thickened. Start adding the oil a drop at a time, whisking well after each drop. When the mixture has thickened, pour in the rest of the grapeseed and olive oils in a slow, steady stream, whisking constantly, until you have a thick mayonnaise texture. You may not need to use all the oil. Stir in the crushed garlic and season to taste with salt, pepper, white wine vinegar, and lemon juice—I like it quite acidic with squid. Add a dash of water if it seems too thick. (You could make it in a food processor or with an electric hand whisk for large quantities.) It will keep in a jar in the fridge for up to a week.

To make the sandwich — Heat the olive oil in a frying pan over low heat, add the onion, and cook, stirring gently, for 10 minutes, or until soft. Season with salt and pepper during cooking. Increase the heat to medium and cook for 5 minutes or so, or until caramelized. Remove and set aside.

Slice the squid tube in half lengthwise. Using a small, sharp knife, score the full length of each piece on both sides. Heat the same pan over medium heat and add a little more olive oil, if needed. Once hot, add the squid and sauté on each side for 1 to 2 minutes. The squid will curl up, so press it down gently with a spatula. Remove the squid from the pan and slice it into even pieces. Spread the lemony aioli on two slices of bread, then divide the squid and caramelized onions between them and add a handful of arugula. Top with the rest of the bread and eat right away.

Chouriço walnut rolls
Pão com chouriço

Makes 6

1 teaspoon/5 g active dried yeast
   or ½ ounce/15 g fresh yeast
1¾ cups/250 g white bread flour,
   plus extra for dusting
¾ cup plus 2 tablespoons/130 g rye flour
1 teaspoon/5 g salt
2 tablespoons/30 ml olive oil, plus extra
   for greasing
2½ ounces/70 g walnuts, toasted and
   coarsely chopped
7 ounces/200 g chouriço (skin removed),
   thinly sliced

Pão com chouriço **is made from a dough mixture dotted with** *chouriço,* **then baked. You can buy it and eat it just as it is from the midnight bakeries that operate around Lisbon after dark, and on a long night out it always gets you going again. This is my version, to which I add chopped walnuts for flavor and crunch.**

You can make this by hand or in a stand mixer with a dough hook. First, dissolve the yeast in a scant cup/230 ml of warm water in a bowl and set it aside for a few minutes until it foams.

Sift in the flours and salt, add the oil, and mix to form a dough. Knead the dough for 10 minutes. Put it in a lightly oiled bowl and cover loosely with plastic wrap. Leave to rise for 6 hours, or overnight, in the fridge.

Turn the dough out onto a lightly floured surface and knead for 5 minutes, then work in the toasted walnuts. Shape the dough into a ball and leave it to rise in a lightly oiled bowl, covered with a kitchen towel, for 2 hours or until doubled in size.

Preheat the oven to 480°F/250°C (convection 445°F/230°C) and dust a baking sheet with flour. Divide the dough into 6 equal pieces. Using your fingers, flatten each portion into a square roughly 4 inches/10 cm across. Arrange 4 or 5 slices of *chouriço* in a vertical line down the middle. Stretch and fold the dough on either side over the *chouriço* like a letter, and pinch it together to seal. Place the rolls seam-side down on the baking sheet and dust them with flour. Bake for 8 minutes, then turn the oven temperature down to 390°F/200°C (convection 355°F/180°C) and bake for another 15 to 20 minutes. Remove and leave to cool on a wire rack. Don't leave them for too long, though—they're best enjoyed warm.

Blood sausage and apple sandwich

Sandes de morcela com maça

Serves 2

For the relish

1 small fennel bulb, trimmed and diced

1 large Granny Smith apple, skin on, diced

1 small shallot, diced

1 small red pepper, seeded and diced

2 tablespoons extra-virgin olive oil,
    plus a little extra to serve

1 tablespoon Chardonnay vinegar or
    other good-quality white wine vinegar

Flaky sea salt and ground white pepper

For the sandwich

6 slices smoked morcela or
    good-quality blood sausage

1 tablespoon olive oil

4 slices Cornbread (page 299), sourdough,
    or other rustic loaf

Here, I am pairing an apple relish with the smoked blood sausage known as *morcela*. Ideally, the relish should be made in advance so that the flavors have time to develop, but you want to cook the *morcela* at the last minute. The fresh, sharp crunch of the raw apple makes a lovely contrast with the rich sausage. For a special occasion, you could adapt the sandwich filling by serving it as little canapés on thin cornbread toasts.

To make the relish — Mix together all the ingredients in a bowl and season with salt and pepper. The flavor of the apple should be quite dominant, so have a taste and add more apple if you think it's needed. Set aside at room temperature to macerate, and taste it again for seasoning before serving.

To make the sandwich — Heat a frying pan over medium heat and brush the *morcela* with olive oil. Add the *morcela* to the hot pan and cook for 3 minutes on each side, or until crisp. Remove and set aside. Toast the bread in the same pan for a few minutes on one side, so it soaks up the cooking juices for extra flavor.

Spoon the relish on top of each slice of cornbread and top with the *morcela*, followed by a drizzle of extra-virgin olive oil. I like to eat this while the *morcela* is still warm and crispy.

Cornbread

Broa

Makes 2 medium loaves

1 teaspoon/5 g active dried yeast
1 teaspoon superfine sugar
3 cups/420 g white bread flour,
     plus extra for dusting
2½ cups/300 g fine yellow cornmeal
1 teaspoon/5 g fine sea salt
2 tablespoons/30 ml butter, melted

Broa is a rich, dense, rustic loaf made with cornmeal, and is traditionally baked in large loaves that keep for a couple of weeks. It's served with many dishes, such as *caldo verde* (page 89), and finds several uses in cooking too, most often in the form of bread crumbs or croutons. It also tastes wonderful simply toasted and spread with butter, soft pork fat, or olive oil.

In a small bowl, dissolve the yeast and sugar in 1 cup/250 ml of warm water and leave to stand for a few minutes until it starts to foam on top. Stir in 1 cup/140 g of the flour and cover with a kitchen towel. Leave in a warm place for 30 to 45 minutes, or until the dough has more or less doubled in size.

Put the cornmeal and salt in the bowl of a stand mixer. Pour in ⅞ cup/200 ml of boiling water and the melted butter and mix with the dough hook until it forms a stiff dough. Pour the risen yeast and flour mixture into the cornmeal dough along with the remaining 2 cups/280 g flour. Knead for 8 minutes, or until it comes together to form an elastic dough. Turn the dough out onto a lightly floured surface and knead it for a couple of minutes by hand. Divide it in half and shape each piece into a ball. Dust the tops with flour and put them on a large baking sheet lined with baking parchment. Leave to rise, covered with a kitchen towel, in a warm place for about 45 minutes, or until doubled in size.

Preheat the oven to 465°F/240°C (convection 430°F/220°C). Pour 7 tablespoons/100 ml of water into a rimmed baking sheet, set a wire rack on top, and put it in the oven. Carefully slide the bread dough, on its tray, onto the wire rack, quickly close the oven door, and bake for 10 minutes. Reduce the temperature to 390°F/200°C (convection 355°F/180°C) and bake for a further 15 minutes, or until cooked through. Transfer to a wire rack to cool.

Eggplant and zucchini piso rolls

Sandes de beringela e courgette com piso

Serves 2

For the piso
½ garlic clove, crushed
A handful of parsley leaves, finely chopped
Finely grated zest of ½ lemon and freshly
squeezed juice (optional)
Flaky sea salt and ground white pepper
3 tablespoons extra-virgin olive oil

For the sandwich
1 small eggplant, cut into diagonal rounds
1 zucchini, cut into diagonal rounds
4 tablespoons extra-virgin olive oil,
plus extra to drizzle
Sea salt and cracked black pepper
2 Sweet Potato Rolls (page 286)
or other soft bread rolls
1 ounce/30 g full-flavored hard cheese,
such as queijo da Ilha, Gruyère, or
Parmesan, shaved
Piri piri oil (page 156), to serve (optional)

You don't find many vegetarian sandwiches in Portugal, so I've come up with my own using eggplant, zucchini, and *piso*, and it's a stunner. You can adapt it according to the seasons, using leafy greens such as chard or kale, tomatoes, grilled onions, wild mushrooms, or even celery root, marinating the vegetables overnight, if you like, with olive oil and seasoning. The cheese can be varied too; I usually use Portuguese *queijo da Ilha*, Gruyère, or Parmesan. A dash of piri piri oil would be a welcome addition.

To make the piso — Pound the garlic, parsley, and lemon zest with a generous pinch of salt and white pepper and a little of the oil in a mortar and pestle. (You could also chop the herbs and garlic by hand or use a food processor.) Stir in the rest of the oil. If you want more acidity, add a little lemon juice to taste, just before serving.

To make the sandwich — Brush the eggplant and zucchini with the olive oil and season with salt and black pepper. If you have time, leave it to marinate for 1 to 2 hours.

Heat a ridged grill pan over medium heat. Add the eggplant and zucchini and cook for 4 minutes on each side, in batches if necessary. Remove the vegetables from the pan and drizzle with some more olive oil. Cut the rolls in half and toast, cut side down, in the same pan until golden brown.

Spread a generous amount of *piso* on each slice of bread, then build the sandwich with alternating layers of vegetables and cheese. Finish with an extra drizzle of *piso* and piri piri oil.

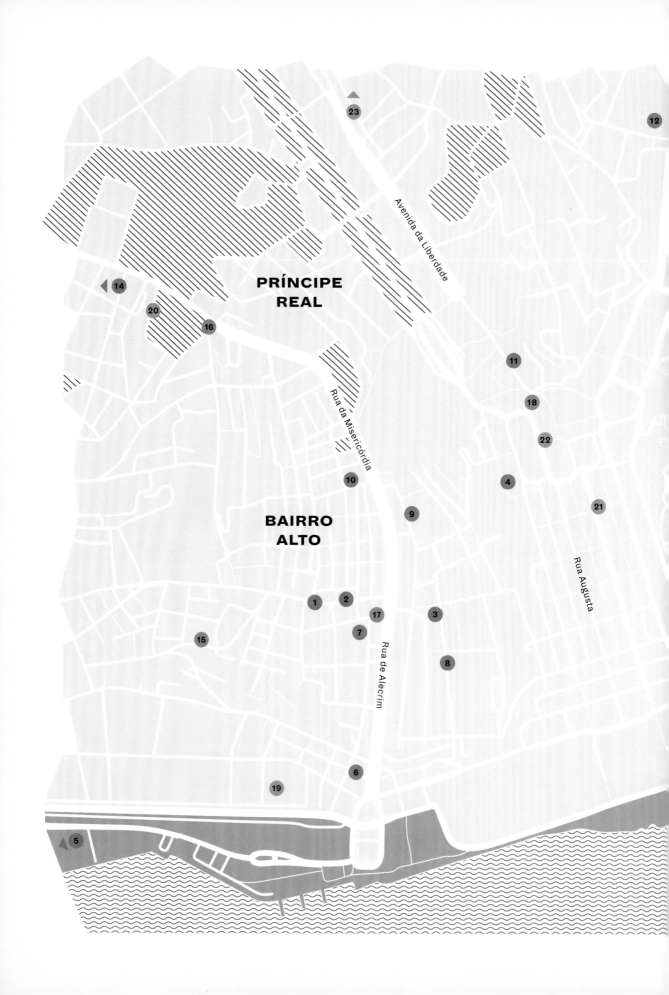

Gazetteer

This map is just the briefest illustration of my favorite cafés, *tascas*, restaurants, food shops, and drinking spots in Lisbon. There have been many exciting new openings in recent years, but here I have focused on the classics. I hope it will be useful as you walk through the streets, uncovering new treasures of your own.

Cafés and pastelarias
1. Chiado Caffe
2. Manteigaria Fábrica de Pastéis de Nata
3. Café A Brasileira
4. Café Nicola and Pastelaria Suiça
5. Pastéis de Belém

Restaurants, tabernas, and tascas
6. Sol e Pesca
7. Taberna da Rua das Flores
8. Belcanto
9. Bairro do Avillez
10. Restaurante Alfaia
11. Gambrinus
12. Ramiro
13. O Cardoso do Estrela de Ouro
14. Stop do Bairro

Bars and quiosques
15. Quiosque do Adamastor
16. Quiosque do Príncipe Real
17. Bairro Alto Hotel Bar
18. A Ginjinha

Food shopping
19. Mercado da Ribeira
20. Mercado Biológico do Príncipe Real
21. Garrafeira Nacional
22. Manteigaria Silva
23. Mercado 31 de Janeiro in Saldanha

See next page for more details →

Cafés and pastelarias

1. Chiado Caffe The *jesuitas* here are simply some of the best in Lisbon—I always pop back before leaving the city to take a box home for the kids.
Rua do Loreto 61

2. Manteigaria Fábrica de Pastéis de Nata These are the best *pastéis*, in my opinion. Come and watch the cooks pipe in the filling, then stand at the counter to wolf a couple down.
Rua do Loreto 2

3. Café A Brasileira This is a time-warp glory, all redwood panels and mirrors and waiters dressed in black and white. A tourist trap? Absolutely, but justifiably so; this is where our national poet Fernando Pessoa took his *bica*. A tip: It is much cheaper inside than on the terrace.
Rua Garrett 120

4. Café Nicola and Pastelaria Suiça This old-school café and nearby *pastelaria* sit on the edge of majestic Rossio Square, and they're great for watching the Lisbon world go by.
Café Nicola, Praça Dom Pedro IV 24–25
Pastelaria Suiça, Praça Dom Pedro IV 96–104

5. Pastéis de Belém The commercial *pastéis de nata* were invented at this place, which is worth a pilgrimage for the blue-and-white tiles and the ambiance alone—even if it's debatable whether they are the very best custard tarts.
Rua Belém 84–92

Restaurants, tabernas, and tascas

6. Sol e Pesca A colorful fishing tackle shop that has become a bar selling all kinds of tinned fish. Open a tin there and then, and eat the contents with bread and a cold glass of wine or beer alongside.
Rua Nova do Carvalho 44

7. Taberna da Rua das Flores One of my treasured places in Lisbon, this cute little *taberna* does really incredible food. The atmosphere is great at night but you'll need to stand in line for a table.
Rua das Flores 103

8. Belcanto This two-Michelin-starred restaurant was a game changer in Lisbon when José Avillez opened it, and it remains one of the best destinations in the city for truly creative food.
Largo de São Carlos 10

9. Bairro do Avillez José Avillez's new restaurant has exciting food, a fun setting, and great drinks. The more casual *taberna* in the front offers cured meats, salads, and other local food that can be eaten on the spot or bought to go.
Rua Nova da Trindade 18

10. Restaurante Alfaia I love this place in funky Bairro Alto for really good, reasonably priced Portuguese food. Sometimes I pop into their shop across the street for *petiscos* and wine.
Travessa da Queimada 22

11. Gambrinus A fabulous old restaurant that gives you the feeling of stepping into a different century. The *pregos* and *croquetes* are some of the best in Lisbon.
Rua das Portas de Santo Antão 23

12. Ramiro The quality at this legendary seafood restaurant is amazing; you need to wait in line but it's worth it. Remember to finish your meal with a *prego*.
Avenida Almirante Reis 1

13. O Cardoso do Estrela de Ouro Along the 28 tram line, in the rather lovely Graça neighborhood, this really is a traditional *tasca*, where Dona Laura and Dona Emilia sing in the kitchen and Senhor Cardoso looks after front of house. Come before noon to taste fresh-fried *salgados* and beat the lunchtime rush.
Rua da Graça 22

14. Stop do Bairro This vibrant little *tasca* is a bit out of the way in Campo de Ourique, but it's near the end of the 28 tram line and worth seeking out. It is decked out with football scarves, but unlike many places in Lisbon it doesn't favor any one team. I like to go and ogle what the people beside me are eating before I order. There are lots of Angolan influences on the menu and the big, yellow-colored homemade fries are to die for. The desserts are also good.
Rua Tenente Ferreira Durão 55A

Bars and quiosques

15. Quiosque do Adamastor This *quiosque* by the Miradouro de Santa Caterina is named after the mythical giant who features in Luís de Camões's famous narrative poem *Os Lusíades*, and you'll find a sculpture of him looking out over the River Tejo. The view from here is great.
Rua de Santa Catarina

16. Quiosque do Príncipe Real I love sitting outside at an old *quiosque* like this on a balmy night, cooling my brow against an ice-cold *porto tónico* or beer before sipping it.
Praça Príncipe Real

17. Bairro Alto Hotel Bar This central hotel has one of the best roof terraces in the entire city, with views out across the river to the statue of Cristo Rei and the Ponte 25 de Abril. They have some lovely wines on offer, but it gets very busy so just be aware that you might have to wait.
Praça Luís de Camões 2

18. A Ginjinha You can try the sweet *ginjinha* liqueur, which is made from sour cherries, in a little shot glass here. Ask for it *com ela* (with a cherry) or *sim ela* (no cherry). It's always bustling with locals, even in the morning.
Largo São Domingos 8

Food shopping

19. Mercado da Ribeira One of the oldest markets in Lisbon, this offers amazing produce at both the market stalls and in the small shops around the perimeter. The market closes at lunchtime but it adjoins the more commercial Time Out food court, which stays open late; the food court boasts *quiosques* from some of the city's big chefs.
Avenida 24 de Julho

20. Mercado Biológico do Príncipe Real This is my favorite farmers' market, right in the center of Lisbon. It's a fantastic place to wander on a Saturday morning.
Jardim do Príncipe Real

21. Garrafeira Nacional A wonderful old shop with a good portfolio of Portugal's best wines.
Rua de Santa Justa 18

22. Manteigaria Silva A great place to buy cured meats from different areas of Portugal. Stand at one of the old barrels eating your selection, or ask for them to vacuum-pack it to go.
Rua Dom Antão De Almada 1

23. Mercado 31 de Janeiro in Saldanha This is a real working market with fabulous characters who have spent a lifetime here selling some of the best fish you'll ever see.
Rua Engenheiro Vieira da Silva

Acknowledgments

This book was made possible by a huge amount of hard work, passion, and perseverance, and the people below are the ones who made it a reality.

My thanks go to: Audrey Gillan for being a force of nature; Andrew Montgomery for the amazing photographs and all the cups of tea; Laoise Casey for being able to translate the strange food language I speak; André Toscano for being there, trying and always striving to help; Célia Pedroso for the enduring support and passion for this project, and also for being a wonderful host; Alice Pedroso for taking me back to childhood and showing me how to make the best *pastéis de massa tenra*; Lucy Pepper for being who you are, the most passionate Portuguese-speaking non-Portuguese person I know, and for saying out loud what many Portuguese are afraid of saying; and Fiona St George and the team at 84 PR for the friendship, guidance, and advice on this and all my projects.

To the wonderful Taberna do Mercado team for believing in Portugal and Portuguese food, and for pushing hard every day to champion this little project. António Galapito for taking the journey with me at Taberna from day one and for making it a huge success; I can't wait for your project in Lisbon, you'll kill it! Turku Zorlutuna for being another force of nature and a great friend; you can really roll with it on any occasion and never get fazed. André Coimbra for being there from the beginning, learning and always being happy to take Taberna forward—I have great expectations of you, my friend! Diana Neto for all the help with the pastries in this book; Bruno Caseiro and Filipa Neto for helping set up Taberna from the start; Thomas Kipling for always being there for support and advice; Luis Chou, Patrick Jahnske, and Jayesh and Rita Patel for believing in Taberna and being patient with me.

To all my other wonderful friends who helped and inspired me during the making of this book:

Paulo Amado for pushing the food scene in Portugal for all these years and for always being a good friend; André Magalhães for the wonderful meals and discussions we had about food and life at the fabulous Taberna da Rua das Flores; Nuno Diniz for all your knowledge about Portuguese food and *enchidos*—many Portuguese chefs have a lot to learn from you; Miguel Pires for the help and advice with the restaurant food and the many bottles of Serradinha; Jorge and João Felizardo for being the brothers that I love and for all the Super Bocks we've shared over the years; Alexandra Prado Coelho, Mónica Bessone, José Avillez, and Luis Lucas.

Thanks to my agent Charlie Brotherstone and to Ed Victor (you will be missed); to Roxanne Newton and to the Chiltern Firehouse team for their patience.

Special thanks to the amazing Bloomsbury team for all their tireless work and belief in me: Xa Shaw Stewart, Natalie Bellos, Richard Atkinson, Lisa Pendreigh, and Lena Hall; in production, Arlene Alexander and Marina Asenjo; in publicity and marketing, Ellen Williams and Sarah Williams. Many thanks also to designer Charlotte Heal and Tegan Hendel, and project editor Laura Gladwin.

Thanks also go to the people who helped with locations and photographs: Luis Miguel and his team of fishermen and -women at Fonte da Telha; Abílio and João at Tasca do Abílio; all at O Cardoso do Estrela de Ouro and Stop do Bairro; Chiara Ferro and her team at Osteria; the family at Leitaria Minhota; the team at Flor da Salva; Jorge Freire at the Lapa apartment where a lot of this book was shot; and Marta Tavares da Silva at the Bairro Alto Hotel for the emergency rooms.

Finally, thank you to the *lisboetas*: the people who make up this wonderful city have such a special place in my heart.

Index

To my grandmother, Albertina, and my father, João, who taught me about food and inspired me to cook, setting me on the path that led to the professional kitchen.

To Clarise for making the *rissóis de camarão* that awakened me to how amazing Portuguese food really is, and made me embark on this journey to capture Lisbon and Portugal, first in a restaurant and now in a book.

To my beautiful children, Orla, Noah, and Finn, whom I love more than anything in this world. I hope to give you this gift of love and passion for Portuguese food and for my native city.